**Dr Hugh Schonfield**, eminent historian and biographer, was born in London and educated at St. Paul's School and Glasgow University. He specialised in Near Eastern Affairs, and was for many years historian of the Suez Canal and contributor on the subject to the Encyclopaedia Brittanica Year Books. Whilst working with the Near East Department of the Ministry of Information during the Second World War, Dr Schonfield also contributed the section on Libya for the government-sponsored volume *Islam Today*. His major interest was in archaeology, especially in the field of Christian origins, and he was one of the scholars who worked on the newly-discovered Dead Sea Scrolls. He was the first Jew to translate the New Testament, a work which received the highest praise for its accuracy and realism from distinguished churchmen and scholars. His best-known work is *The Passover Plot*, of which more than three million copies have been sold. He wrote over thirty books, including *An Old Hebrew Text of St. Matthew's Gospel, The History of Jewish Christianity, According to the Hebrews: A New Translation of the Toldoth Jeshu* and *Proclaiming the Messiah: The Life and Letters of Paul of Tarsus*.

He was President of the Commonwealth of World Citizens and of the International Arbitration League, and was nominated for the Nobel Peace Prize for his services towards international co-operation.

*The Mystery of the Messiah* clarifies the meaning of the terms 'Messiah' and 'Messianic', and in the process provides an informative survey of the ancient history of Israel. The book attempts to link the prophetic with the historical and show that there is a divine purpose at work in the history of mankind. Placing Jesus firmly among his own people and background, *The Mystery of the Messiah* is inspired throughout by Schonfield's lifelong quest for the historical truth about Jesus and his actual religious beliefs.

Schonfield worked on *The Mystery of the Messiah* some eighteen months before his death in January 1988, and it is now published posthumously.

'Here is the final, grand synthesis of Hugh J. Schonfield's decades of imaginative study and deep thinking. On display in these pages is Schonfield the biblical theologian as well as Schonfield the philosopher of history. *The Mystery of the Messiah* is at once a fine introduction to the apocalyptic matrix from which the original Jesus movement emerged and a history of the broader messianic ideal in Judaism. Schonfield offers a constructive vision of socio-religious engagement to create a better, 'Messianic' world. Especially intriguing are the glimpses of the author's own life. Introduced to the New Testament by the Christadelphian sect, Schonfield went on to re-create a living Jewish Jesus-messianism and indeed to undertake near messianic tasks himself, for which he was nominated for the Nobel Peace Prize. Hugh Schonfield was a remarkable man ...... historian and a historic figure. *The Mystery of the Messiah* reveals him as a ....... eitzer.'

Dr Robert M. Price, Editor, *Journal of Higher Criticism*, I ......
Drew University, Madison, New J......

## Selected works by Hugh J. Schonfield

### The Original New Testament
Firethorn Press, an imprint of Waterstone & Co Ltd., London, 1985; distributed by
Sidgwick & Jackson Ltd. New edition by Element Books.

### The Passover Plot
Element Books, mass market edition, 1996; first published by Hutchinson, 1965.

### The Pentecost Revolution
Element Books, 1985; first published by Hutchinson, 1974. Published in USA as
*The Jesus Party.*

### Those Incredible Christians
Element Books, 1985; first published by Hutchinson, 1968.

### After the Cross
A S Barnes & Co., USA., 1981.

### The Essene Odyssey
Element Books, third impression 1993.

### Proclaiming the Messiah:
*The Life and Letters of Paul of Tarsus, Envoy to the Nations*
Open Gate Press, London, 1997.

# The Mystery of the Messiah

*Moses* by Max Sokol (1895-1973).
'The Giving of the Law', the universal foundation of Jewish Christian aspirations,
celebrated at Pentecost.

# The Mystery of
# the Messiah

## Hugh J. Schonfield

OPEN GATE PRESS
LONDON

First published in 1998 by Open Gate Press
51 Achilles Road, London NW6 1DZ

**British Library Cataloguing-in-Publication Programme**
A catalogue record for this book is available from the British Library.

ISBN 1 871871 38 7

Printed in Great Britain by
Redwood Books, Trowbridge, Wiltshire

# Contents

# Introduction

For almost nineteen centuries Christians have been misled and misguided about the origins and nature of their beliefs. The reasons for this will be made clear in the body of this book, which is the outcome of a lifetime of concerned research. Inevitably the sources used are not confined to the Bible. They embrace all that is to be learned from Jewish, Greek and Roman records which throw light on the history of the period and the climate of religious and political thought in which Christianity originated. While not as complete as we would wish, the records now available are very substantial and illuminating, and they ought to be much more familiar than they are to the man-in-the-pew. Unfortunately, one of the reasons that they are not is that Christian spokesmen are concerned to suppress them.

A fundamental fact is that Christianity did not begin as a new religion or even as a religion at all. In its inception it was a Jewish patriotic movement whose adherents claimed that the ultimate king and deliverer of Israel had manifested himself in a contemporary descendant of King David called Joshua (Jesus in Greek). He had presented himself as the Messiah (Christ in Greek), "the anointed" ruler of Israel. Such a person, as we shall discover, was awaited at the time by the Jews, more especially as their country was occupied and ruled by the Romans. But in those days his function went far beyond the deliverance of Israel. The deliverance was essential, because faithful Israel was destined to be the means by which all the nations would cease from idolatry and worship the One God. Under the King Messiah and his people they would come to learn the ways of peace and justice; and for this purpose their representatives would need to travel to a liberated and redeemed Israel. Without this ideology, fundamental with the early Christians, there was no point or purpose in describing them as Christian.

1

In Israel the Christians were known as *Notsrim* (Nazoreans), meaning custodians or preservers. They created an organization largely borrowed from another Messianic-minded body of the period, known as the Essenes, with which they had much in common. Until AD 66 the headquarters of the Christians was Jerusalem. They had a Council, which included the Envoys (Apostles) Jesus had chosen, and their President was Jacob (James), the younger brother of Jesus next in age. To this Council all communities (churches) of Christians outside Israel were obliged to report, and envoys, Paul among them (*Acts* xviii.21, xx.16). The principal Jewish festival of the Essenes, which became that of the Christians, was Pentecost, and it was at this festival that reports were submitted and matters affecting individuals and communities were dealt with.

There was, in fact, a completely different set-up to what Christians of later times have conceived. Primitive Christianity was Jewish through and through. As I have said, it did not begin as a religion but as a Messianic movement within Israel. The adherents were all loyal to the Jewish faith (*Acts* vi.7, xxi.20-26). And, since their number included those who had companied with Jesus, it is certain that Judaism was his own religion and that in no respect had he departed from it either in what he represented himself to be or in what he taught. Indeed, if he claimed to be the Messiah (the Christ) it could not be otherwise. He must be the living exemplar of the Laws of Moses governing his people. The words of Isaiah (ix.6), "the government shall be on his shoulder" was interpreted as "the Messiah has taken the Law (*Torah*) upon himself to keep it".

How, then, did the transformation come about which alienated Jesus from his people, paganized him, and turned Christianity into a new semi-heathen religion?

This is a vital question, which will require treatment at length in the appropriate place. But we may indicate here certain contributory factors. One was the "opening of the door of faith" to non-Jews. This was not contrary to the Messianic design, for it had been predicted that the Messianic nation would be "a light to the Gentiles" (*Isa*. xlix. 6), and "declare my [God's] glory among the Gentiles" (*Isa*. lxvi.19). Paul had regarded this activity as the mission entrusted to him, and used considerable rabbinical exegesis to demonstrate that Gentiles who became subjects of the Messiah as king of Israel were thereby made naturalised Israelites and thus ceased to be Gentiles (*Rom*. xi, *Gal*. iii.29, *Eph*. ii.11-13), on grounds of faith not of birth.

Unfortunately, many such converted Gentiles were hostile to the Jews. There was much rivalry and contention between Greeks and Jews in many parts of the Roman Empire, and this affected many Christian communities, especially when the Jews lost their war with the Romans in AD 70. By this time Paul and his generation were dead, and surviving members of the central Christian government had been forced to flee from Jerusalem into asylum in parts of Syria under the leadership of Simeon, a first cousin of Jesus. The ex-Gentile Christians were now without leadership, and because of their anti-Roman views the Roman government regarded them as just as much rebels as the Jewish militants. Both were Messianists, seeking to substitute the Kingdom of God on Earth for the Roman Empire. Among the religions of the Empire, Judaism was acknowledged officially, because in the Provinces the Jewish communities had been found to be good and law-abiding citizens, and not at all in league with the militants in Galilee and Judea, whose activities they resented (*Acts* xvii.6-7). But the Romans refused now to grant the non-Jewish Christians recognition as a distinct religion, even when their communities denied their Jewishness and created a paganised Christianity. For the Romans they were still ill-wishers of the Empire finding supporters among the slave population. The truth about all the circumstances is very different to what the Church has depicted.

After the defeat of the Jews by the Romans and the exile of the Christian government at Jerusalem, the Christians in other lands were left with uncertain and inadequate knowledge of the views and experiences of Jesus as Messiah. Written records were needed, and it was in the period after AD 72 that written Gospels were composed in various parts of the Roman Empire. Reliable information being inadequate, and a paganization of Jesus being now required by non-Jews, the Gospel accounts were largely fictionalized, depending on where and by whom they were composed. Two of the Gospels in the New Testament, *Matthew* and *Luke*, did have in *Mark* a partially reliable source, and another which scholars have called Q. But inevitably and progressively Jesus was alienated from his people and deified. In the New Testament this comes out especially in the latest of the Gospels, *John*, which is why it has had the greatest appeal to a Gentilised Church.

From the second century AD onwards, the significance of the Messianic in its original sense progressively disappeared. The "times of the Gentiles" (*Lk.* xxi.24) had begun. This was confirmed when

3

Christianity joined forces with its former enemy Rome. The Church's creeds were created by Jew-haters, with inevitable consequences. The story down the centuries would embrace the Crusades, the Holy Roman Empire, the Holy Inquisition, the pogroms, the Nazis.

But in the nineteenth century the first signs began to appear that the Messianic would come back into its own, and these signs have progressively been increasing. We may list here a number of them. The restoration to Jews of civic rights in Christian countries, the study of the Bible objectively as a collection of ancient documents rather than as the infallible Word of God, the increase of archaeological research in Bible lands, the chance discovery of writings and objects long lost which would throw new light on Christian beginnings and chronology, the editing and publication of Jewish apocryphal and apocalyptic literature from immediately before and after the time of Jesus, the developing sense of End of Time and Second Adventist convictions among Christian nonconformist denominations, encouraging increased missionary activity. On the Jewish side there was the growing Zionist Movement, which in the First World War prompted the British government to proclaim Palestine as the Jewish National Home, and which would be crowned by the creation of the State of Israel. With this transformation, the place of Jesus in Jewish history gained recognition, and Jewish scholars could now devote themselves without discomfort to the New Testament period. There were signs of a new relationship between Christians and Jews in the formation of societies for mutual religious exploration. The Roman Church so far changed course that the Second Vatican Council declared that, "No ancestral or collective blame can be imputed to the Jews as a people for what happened in Christ's Passion." As I write, the present Pope has been the first to participate in worship in a Jewish synagogue (13. 4. 86), and to speak of the Jews as "our elder brethren".

In a secular context, political and scientific, the changes within my own lifetime – I was born in 1901 – have been tremendous, creating a new planetary perspective. In spite of great wars and threats of a nuclear holocaust, the sense of our world as a whole, and as a governed whole, has been taking positive effect.

At the dawn of the twentieth century there was a movement towards the recognition of World Law symbolised in the Peace Palace at The Hague; and this had been encouraged by rapid communication links by land and sea. This would advance after World War I to the formation of the League of Nations, and after World War II to the United Nations, and would begin to foster a sense of planetary responsibility and world citizenship. At the same time we were only beginning to know our planet as a whole, by exploration of the poles and areas previously uncharted. The conquest of the air was now upon us, still further making the Earth a smaller place; and then rocket flight would enable us for the first time actually to see our world whole from outside. We set foot on the moon, and could begin to plant stations in space. We could even send instruments into the deeper regions of the solar system.

Rapidity of communication became intensified by fresh inventions, and now we also faced problems of food and energy. We had to intensify a planetary outlook, concern for the world's resources and the distribution of food and minerals. Both human beings and animals were a world responsibility of the human race. The transformation of the world scene in less than a century had been tremendous, and we could not know what mightier changes would speedily be in store.

All that I have outlined, and touched upon briefly, convey to my mind that our Earth is serving some experimental purpose for which we have been placed here. Our conditions are special ones within the solar system, and the pace at which we are progressing towards our goal has been speeding up through the ages.

What the ultimate destiny of mankind will be is not yet evident. But the Messianic, as a kind of prophetic blueprint, has indicated a peaceful world order, a Heaven on Earth. Unlike what the Church teaches, the Bible is not about going to Heaven, but of Heaven coming to us.

It has been supposed by multitudes of various Faiths down the centuries that human existence on Earth was a preparation for some individual hereafter, good or bad, as might be merited. Since each of us is a person in his or her own right, the accent has been upon the individual rather than upon the collective, on what is going to happen to *me*. There is a justification for this, but only if we see it in correct perspective, recognising that every individual is a miniature collective. Each of us, as has scientifically been remarked, is a colony of animals. Every person's brain functions as a world government.

Has not the individual always been related to the collective? The group and the tribe were not invented by man: they exist and function in all creatures. But man has increased the variety of his associations and disciplines, many of them directed to contributing towards understanding and advancement. This phenomenon, as we have become aware, is an ingredient of a cosmos which we have had nothing to do with creating; and consequently there are material grounds for supposing that intention in us is evidential of intention beyond our choosing in which we are involved. It has always been an absurdity to me that chance should give rise to design, and accident to purposefulness.

Supposing that the instruments and machines we make were endowed with a higher degree of consciousness than has been practicable so far, an intelligence and reasoning capacity. Would they be able to infer the existence of Man? They have a brain of sorts which enables them to respond to our signals over vast distances. It would not take much more for them to be conscious of a Signaller. Already in our science fiction stories we are relating Man to Machine in a manner which religion has stated functions between the divine and the human.

We take it as a matter of course that in our relationships with other humans, with animals, and with machines, we exercise Guidance. And this is an indication of another capacity, that of Purposefulness. Why are these endowments part of our composition? There must surely be some advantage, some development, which it is needful to obtain from their employment. And we have every right to infer that this holds good in the universe at large.

In many ways, it would seem, we are slowly learning more about God by becoming gods; and this takes us right back in the Bible to the book of *Genesis* where Adam was seen to have god-like qualities, to be Son of God, made in the image of God.

Thousands of years ago it came home (or was revealed) to a part of mankind that our planet was related to a special purpose, the nature of which was corporate and collective. Insight into that purpose lent to it also direction and objectivity, since there was available a kind of blueprint, though this was not always intelligible and decipherable. We may call it the Messianic.

Today we can delve rather more deeply and accurately into the Messianic Mystery than was formerly practicable, because we are at the beginning of a period when greater knowledge will be indispensable. We must face that the discarding of many cherished convictions will be involved, especially by Christians, who are nominally the Messianists, but who very early on became alien to the character and requirements of the Messianic programme.

# 1
# *Approach to the Mystery*

The Messianic Mystery, as I have conveyed, is of great moment for mankind, and it is not a difficult one to unravel and comprehend once sufficient liberty of mind has been gained to identify with its implications. The problems are different for Jews and for non-Jews, and for theists and atheists. Those who might chiefly have been expected to provide clarification, the Christians, are those who have been responsible for a great deal of misinterpretation, and they perhaps, may be the hardest to convince. It may even be said that the Church has an innate antipathy to the true nature of the Messianic, because this is in fundamental conflict with Christianity as a religion.

Initially Christianity was not a religion. It only became one when it was divorced from its Jewish roots. It was what we would describe today as an ideology, one that was unique in type and objectives. It involved a purpose for our planet. It had to do with God, but not with any theology. It had political aims without being a political system. It sought fulfilment not by means of force but by means of service. It took for its inspiration what many would reject rather than seek after, and found its motivation in love instead of hatred and antagonism.

As I have pointed out in the Introduction, the Greek term 'Christ' is a translation of the Hebrew term 'Messiah', both meaning 'the anointed one'. In Israel high priests and kings were anointed with oil when called to office, signifying their consecration. The Messiah would be Israel's ultimate monarch, setting an example to his people as they would serve as an example to mankind. The circumstances are to be found in the Bible, in the closing chapters of the book of

7

*Exodus* and in the books of *Samuel*. Thus the Greek version of the Old Testament (the Septuagint) can employ the term christ (*christos*) in a descriptive sense long before and without reference to Jesus. But when Jesus was proclaimed as Christ to Greek-speaking Jews of the Mediterranean world they would know at once that this meant that the ultimate king of Israel appointed by God had manifested himself. For Jews no matter of deity was involved in this description of Jesus as 'the Christ', 'the anointed one', even though in Israel it could be said of kings that they were under guidance by God as of a father with his son.

But *Christos* could not convey to Gentiles what it conveyed to Jews. They would therefore sometimes refer to *Chrestos*, a proper name meaning 'useful' or 'beneficial', or they would have him referred to as Jesus Christ, dropping the definite article and treating Christ as if it was a descriptive surname applying to a god. It was all too easy for a Gentile to think of Jesus as divine when told that he was a king; for not only did they hold that gods could appear on Earth in human form (*Acts* xiv.12-13), they also invested royalty with deity (*Acts* xii. 22), so that the Pharaohs were "sons of Jupiter". Alexander the Great, it was said, was not the son of Philip of Macedon; he was born of the god who had intercourse with his mother. It would come naturally to a Gentile that if Jesus was a king he was also a god, son of the God of the Jews, who had fertilised the womb of his mother.

It should, therefore, be no matter of surprise that the general and non-Jewish view of what the Messianic represents, as expounded by the Christian religion, should be an amalgam of the Jewish and the pagan. This comes out clearly where the common man is concerned, and he can use an expletive like "Jesus Christ Almighty!"

But because Christianity in its development turned Messianism into a quasi-pagan religion with an elaborate theology and ritual, powered by an overwhelming sense of obligation to a god who sacrificed himself in human guise for human sin, this does not mean that Judaism in its own progression has been more faithful to the Messianic. In its objectives the Messianic was designed to overcome the barriers of race and religion, not to exalt one part of mankind over another. And certainly there is a sacrificial element in it, though of another kind to what Christians have imagined.

We can learn much about this ideology from the Bible. One may indeed say that the Messianic is the Bible's theme. The ancient rabbis claimed that when in *Genesis* it is said "the wind of God ruffled the surface of the (primeval) waters" (*Gen.* i. 2), that was the Spirit of Messiah. The Messianic purpose was there from the infancy of our planet.

We may indeed say that the Messianic is intimately related to the purpose for which our planet was designed, and holds within it one part of the secret of human destiny. For this reason we have to follow its evolution as communicated in the past by vision operating in the context of history. There has to get through to us a sense of destiny, of purpose, the God's eye view of Earth's function, mediated through the images and concepts of individuals of successive epochs, but also reflecting the limitations of their knowledge.

The Jewish sages of old were right in apprehending that the equipment of Earth for the advent of Man was not a matter of accident or chance. All the resources for which Man would stand in need as he developed were there ages before his appearance. Only at a late juncture did *homo sapiens* emerge, Man in his imaginative and planning capacity. This is what the Bible depicts as Man made in the image of God, Man as Son of God (*Lk.* iii. 38), equipped with supermundane qualities. The Divine was all-embracing, and therefore the Bible uses for this a comprehensive term, *Elohim* (the Powers-that-be). The evolutionary process is focused on a particular family in the Bible exposition, the Adamites, which in course of time would give rise to a nation whose function would be unlike any other, and which collectively would be Son of God (*Exod.* iv. 22-23).

We should spell this out. Moses is told by God to say to mighty Pharaoh, "Israel is my Son, my Firstborn. And I say to you, 'Let my Son go that he may serve me.'" The Christian may never have considered that the people of Israel (as Messiah collective) is described in the same way as is Jesus (as Messiah singular). In neither case did the term Son of God imply deity. This was posited as regards Jesus by the Church when it became paganised. But if it was proper to take it literally, why do not Christians worship Israel?

What has to be clarified and appreciated is that the Bible presents us not only with an individual Messiah, but also essentially with a Messiah-collective. The Messiahship is shared (*Hos.* xi. 1; *Mt.* ii. 15). The Nation-Messiah would have to be singular among the nations, set apart for the service and benefit of all peoples, and as a mediator between God and Mankind.

So, when Abraham, the progenitor, was called to Canaan from

Chaldea, he was told: "In thee shall all families of the Earth be bless-ed" (*Gen.* xii.3). The promise is reiterated that the nation arising from Abraham's descendants would be for the blessing of all na-tions. It will be agreed that this is a very exceptional reason for a nation's existence.

Here is no lust for conquest or tribal egoism. The function of this nation is to serve and to bless, to operate in a priestly capacity, performing as a mediator for the nation-states.

But for such a purpose a severe training and discipline was called for, a priestly code of national conduct, the experience of slavery, as in Egypt, and of homelessness, as in the wanderings in the Wilderness.

The Messianic requires us to read and study the books of Moses with a new appreciation and insight, not as something relating to a past experience which has been superseded, but as something of present and future relevance to that ideal world economy which would come to be expressed as the Kingdom or rule of God on Earth.

# 2

# *A Holy Nation*

The Messianic Plan in embryo is represented in the Song of Moses, the statesman-prophet, in *Deuteronomy* xxxii.

> When the Most High divided to the nations their inheritance,
> When he separated the sons of men,
> He set the bounds of the peoples
> According to the number of the Children of Israel.
> For the Lord's portion is his people;
> Jacob is the lot of his inheritance.

Part of the sense of this passage is easy to follow. In dividing up the goodly heritage of the Earth among the nations God reserved the people of Israel as his own share. The dedication to God of the first-born, and the first fruits of produce, as a token that all things come from his bounty, is one of the oldest religious customs. Here it is claimed that God has accepted one nation from among all the others as dedicated to him. It might be put another way, that Israel is the ground rent which the nations pay to God for their tenure of the Earth.

The figure of Israel as the first-born, which occurs frequently in the Bible, has this implication among others, conveying the setting apart of this people for the Divine service.

The heathen seer Balaam, sent by Balak his sovereign to curse Israel, looking down from the heights upon the tents of Israel pitched in their symbolic order around the Tent of Meeting, is made to cry:

> How shall I curse, whom God hath not cursed?
> Or how shall I defy, whom the Lord hath not defied?
> From the top of the rocks I see him,
> And from the hills I behold him.
> Lo, this people shall dwell alone,
> And shall not be reckoned among the nations.

11

Who can count the dust of Jacob,
And the number of the fourth part of Israel?
Let me die the death of the righteous,
And let my last end be like his! (*Num.* xxiii. 8-10)

The singularity of the status of Israel is here strikingly described, "a people dwelling alone, not reckoned among the nations". We have the unique distinction of Jews from Gentiles (the nations in general), not in any exalted sense, but in a priestly sense. God declares to Israel through Moses: "Now, therefore, if ye will obey my voice indeed, and keep my covenant, then shall ye be unto me a special possession from among all peoples – for all the Earth is mine – and ye shall be unto me a kingdom of priests, and an holy nation" (*Exod.* xix. 5-6).

The convocation at Sinai, and the giving of the Law, had as their stated object the preparation and equipment of this people for its priestly Messianic vocation. This could only dimly be apprehended at the time, "Ye shall be holy unto me: for I the Lord am holy, and have severed you from other people, that ye should be mine" (*Lev.* xx. 26).

The economy of Israel in the Wilderness plainly appears as a microcosm where within the camp the Twelve Tribes answer to the nations, the priestly tribe of Levi to Israel, and the Tent of Meeting to the presence of God with Israel. This is confirmed by the ordinances governing the Levites. Called out and sanctified from the other tribes they offer a demonstration of the role of Israel in the world of nations.

When the commandment was given to "take the sum of all the congregation of Israel" (*Num.* i. 2), the tribe of Levi was specifically omitted from this census. Levi was not to be numbered: it was appointed as the intermediary between God and Israel, and its encampment was to be pitched round about the Tent of Meeting (the Tabernacle) as a tribe dwelling alone, not reckoned among the tribes of Israel.

In the same way as in the wider context of Israel among the nations, so within Israel the Levites were separated to be God's possession. "The Lord spake unto Moses, saying, 'And I, behold, I have taken the Levites from among the Children of Israel instead of all the firstborn… among the Children of Israel: therefore the Levites shall be mine; because all the firstborn are mine'" (*Num.*iii.11-13). The Levitic tribe was dedicated solely to the Divine service: in this capacity supra-territorial, and required to bless the people in God's name, as – under the covenant with Abraham – Israel was to bless all nations. Ultimately Israel would reside in a Holy Land as in a Temple.

> At that time the Lord separated the tribe of Levi... to stand before the Lord to minister unto him, and to bless in his name, unto this day. Wherefore Levi hath no part nor inheritance with his brethren; the Lord is his inheritance, according as the Lord thy God promised him. (*Deut.* x. 8-9)

The description which the Pentateuch gives of the encampment of Israel in the wilderness makes it clear that we are looking at a symbolic scale model of the world economy. Central in the scheme is the Tent of Meeting, for the spiritual must be central in any durable world order, as the soul in the body politic. In close association with the Tabernacle, and mediating the will of God to the surrounding tribes, are the holy Levites – the exterritorial tribe. "The Children of Israel shall pitch their tents, every man by his own camp, and every man by his own standard, throughout their hosts. But the Levites shall pitch round about the Tabernacle of Testimony, that there be no wrath upon the congregation of the Children of Israel" (*Num.* i. 52-53).

The twelve tribes themselves are disposed in world-quarter groups of three, north, south, east and west of the Tabernacle (*Num.* ii), an arrangement which enables us more fully to comprehend the meaning of the words:

> When the Most High divided to the nations their inheritance,
> When he separated the sons of men,
> He set the bounds of the peoples
> According to the number of the Children of Israel.

Thus the concept of Israel as the Messianic Nation is plainly set down in the Books of Moses, and the theme is continued in the writings of the Prophets. A notable passage in *Isaiah* proclaims: "Thou, Israel, art my servant, Jacob, whom I have chosen, the seed of Abraham my friend. Thou whom I have taken from the ends of the Earth, and called thee from the chief men thereof, and said unto thee, 'Thou art my servant; I have chosen thee, and not cast thee away'" (*Isa.* xli. 8-9).

It is most unfortunate that Christians, for the most part, read only those passages of the Bible which suit their ideas, and consequently have quite a false image of what it teaches.

God does not make mistakes. He would not have chosen Israel for

13

his purposes if at any time or for any reason he was ready to reject them. Paul, who regarded himself as apostle to the Gentiles, stressed this as much as anyone. "I say then, hath God cast away his people? God forbid... God hath not cast away his people which he foreknew" (*Rom.* xi). Many Christian authorities, in their antisemitism, have claimed the contrary, violating the teaching of the Bible, and being in fact almost totally ignorant of the real nature of Christianity.

It is very hard for non-Jews to master the Messianic as their tradition is so different. Hence that famous couplet by a Christian divine: "How odd of God to choose the Jews." It has to be worked at by Christians, and for a reason relating to their true status, namely their identity with the people of Israel. Apart from Israel the Church has no validity. Consequently the Christian not of Jewish stock has every justification – indeed necessity – to study the story of Israel in the Scriptures as reflecting the Church's own nature, history and purpose.

As a beginning the Christian should take note that what he describes as the Old Testament was the Bible of Jesus, which he accepted totally as God's Word. Consequently he was fully committed to the Messianic function of Israel as related in it with which his own mission was totally intertwined. It could not be otherwise, because Israel *was* the Church (*Acts* vii. 38), and to no other people than Israel did the Messianic apply. Had it been otherwise, and had Jesus been divine, as pagan-minded Christians proclaim, he would have made sure that he was not born a Jew.

The Messianic has to be regained and accepted by the Church as the true expression of the reason for its existence, its identity with the People of Israel. In the nature of things there never could be any other than the one People of God, in which Gentiles converted from paganism could have a part as naturalised Israelites (*I. Pet.* ii. 9-10). Paul had made this clear in *Romans* xi, the grafting of the wild olive branches into the stem of the cultivated olive tree of Israel. And as he wrote to the Ephesian converts, "Remember, that ye being *in time past Gentiles...* that at that time ye were without Christ [the Messiah], being aliens from the Commonwealth of Israel, and strangers to the Covenants of Promise... But now in Christ Jesus ye who previously were far off are made nigh by the blood of Christ... Now therefore ye are no more strangers and foreigners, but fellow-citizens with the saints [of Israel], and of the household of God" (*Eph.* ii.11-13, 19).

For non-Jews, becoming a Christian involves becoming an Israelite. There is no getting round this. The Christian has therefore to study the history and function of Israel, and this not as relating to some other body of people.

We must argue this out, because it is fundamental to our understanding of God's plan for mankind. It is of Israel that it was written, "Behold my servant, whom I uphold; mine elect, in whom my soul delighteth; I have put my spirit upon him: he shall bring forth judgment to the nations [Gentiles]... He shall not fail nor be discouraged, till he have set judgment in the Earth: and the isles shall wait for his law" (*Isa.* xlii.1, 4).

One must continually stress that the choice of Israel was not a matter of Divine favouritism. It was a choice for a very dedicated and arduous function, demanding great discipline, and entailing much suffering. It was for that reason that the Law of Moses was given. And very early on, as we shall note, the Israelites were keen to opt out of the responsibilities laid upon them. At the root of these there had to be love, love for all mankind, love for the foreigner, as taught in the revelation to Moses, the source from which Jesus learnt. Specifically it was laid down: "The foreigner that dwelleth with you shall be unto you as one born among you, and thou shalt love him as thyself; for ye were foreigners in the land of Egypt" (*Lev.* xix.34).

The failure of Israel in Bible times to devote itself to its Messianic function was not held to relieve it of its mission. The national must pass through the refining fires of judgment to its reconsecration. To this end a new covenant would be brought into operation, more intimate than the old, to secure the high ends always in view. "Behold, the days come, saith the Lord, when I will make a new covenant with the house of Israel, and with the house of Judah: not according to the covenant that I made with their fathers in the day that I took them by the hand to bring them out of the land of Egypt; which my covenant they brake... But this shall be the covenant that I will make with the house of Israel; after those days, saith the Lord, I will put my Law in their inward parts, and write it in their hearts... For I will forgive their iniquity, and I will remember their sin no more" (*Jer.* xxxi.31-34).

The Christian should know that the New Covenant (the same as New Testament) is not to be with another people, but with the people of Israel. Neither is it to be with the adherents of a new religion. The New Covenant is with the Jewish nation, for only this nation was set apart for the Messianic function. 'New' does not mean that the Covenant is one of another kind, superseding the previous one. The terms are the same, but they make the previous Covenant more capable of realization by its terms being lodged in each person's heart and mind.

There never was any question of an exchange of one People of God for another. "Thus saith the Lord which giveth the sun for a light by day, and the ordinances of the moon and of the stars for a light by night... If those ordinances depart from before me, saith the Lord, then the seed of Israel also shall cease from being a nation before me for ever. Thus saith the Lord: If Heaven above can be measured, and the foundations of the Earth searched out beneath, I will also cast off all the seed of Israel for all they have done" (*Jer.* xxxi.35-37). In other words, for the prophet, God was propounding the impossible as regards his exchange of Israel for any other body of people. If Christians hold that *they* are the People of God, it can only be if they acknowledge themselves as members of the House of Israel.

Certainly, as we have already pointed out, there was indicated an enlargement of the nation of Israel. "The Lord God which gathereth the outcasts of Israel saith, 'Yet I will gather others to him, beside those who are gathered unto him'" (*Isa.* lvi.8). Not only Israelites by race, but Israelites by naturalization and by faith, will ultimately form the holy nation, and priestly kingdom. "I will send those that escape of them [i.e. of Israel] to the nations... that have not heard my fame, neither have seen my glory; and they shall declare my glory [that of the One God in Unity] among the nations... And I will also take of them for priests and for Levites, saith the Lord" (*Isa.* lxvi.19-21).

Here, in these post-exilic predictions, the Messianic nation begins to assume a more comprehensive character. By faith in the God of Israel non-Jews can become Israelites, thereby ceasing to be Gentiles and taking upon themselves the responsibilities of Israel's world mission. It was this Jewish teaching that strongly influenced the Apostle Paul in carrying the Messianic message to Gentiles, members of the heathen nations.

If the Church had not become unfaithful it would have continued to teach that the Gentile who becomes a Christian changes his nationality. He joins the Jewish people as a member of the House of Israel. Failure to retain this position has already delayed the coming of the Kingdom of God on Earth by nineteen centuries.

Previously, the natural Israel had rightly been castigated by its prophets for failure to be faithful to the Divine calling. But it was never abandoned as the People of God; and there was at all times a loyal remnant. The Gentilised Church was very ready to denounce the Jews, and claim that God had cast them off, and that the non-Jewish Church was the new People of God. Such was the force of antisemitism. What should have been apprehended by now is that the Catholic Church throughout its own history had acted in an infinitely worse manner than anything recorded of the Jewish People. Its slanders, paganisms, tortures and massacres, would cry to high Heaven; so that if any people was to be abandoned and cast off it should be the Christians. Catholics and Protestants are still murdering one another in Northern Ireland.

It would appear that Christians, while down on the Jews, do not want to know about *Romans* xi.21-22, where there is a very clear reference to the casting away of Gentile Christians if they fail to honour their responsibilities as members of the People of God which is Israel.

Let us begin to apprehend from reading the Bible what great demands, what unique demands, were being made in conferring on Israel its singular status as a priestly nation. Where there is the consciousness of such a vocation there has to be a willingness for self-dedication, for the acceptance of many restrictions on one's way of life, for readiness to be different. This calls for much prayer and heart-searching.

The Israel which spent forty years in the wilderness was still a youth when its destiny was revealed, with all the fires of youth. Left to itself it had no wish to be singular, to cut itself off from the pleasures and pursuits of its neighbours, the nations in general. It wanted to go to war, to indulge in sports and orgies, like everyone else. In the event, Israel committed itself to a status of which it did not fully appreciate the implications and consequences, and for which it was far from ready.

This cannot be said for converts from the Gentiles, who cannot offer any excuse with the Bible in their hands, and the evidences of the Church's sorry story. They should heed Paul's words: "On them which fell (of the natural Israel), severity; but towards thee, goodness, if thou continue in his goodness; otherwise thou also shalt be cut off."

17

# 3

# *Enter a King*

When Israel was called to Messianic office its station and function was of a priestly order. The problems arising from this peculiar kind of nationhood were not too grave, but serious enough, while on the move, following a Bedouin kind of existence. But once there was settlement in the Promised Land the circumstances were very different. There was the experience of nationhood in a civic and political sense, the business of living as a self-governing community. There were all the problems arising from relationships with the already settled populations, to be resolved by conflict or by close communication. There were the attractions of the Nature Cults of farming peoples, and the effects of having possessions, commerce and the acquisition of wealth. Almost everything was in enticing divergence from the dedication demanded of a priestly nation.

We can read of these circumstances in the Bible, in the books of *Joshua*, *Judges* and *I. Samuel*. And the circumstances are brought home to us more emphatically by what archaeology has unearthed, of towns and inscriptions, images and artefacts.

The status of a priestly nation speedily took a back seat, and the worldly largely took over. It was found that the spiritual could increasingly be left to those set aside for this ministry, as the Levites were, and a new structure of government was created for secular matters. They could not, of course, be divorced, and a way had to be constructed for distinguishing, while still combining, the spiritual and the secular. Something similar was to happen in the Middle Ages in the concept of the Holy Roman Empire. With Israel, the nation delegated being a "Kingdom of Priests" to its own priestly tribe, and called for all practical purposes for a Sovereign State ruled by a lay monarch. But since the ruler in the sphere of government exercised some of the qualities of deity, it was all too easy to regard him literally

18

as the national god's son and representative. This applied especially to societies which accepted that deities could appear on Earth in human form.

There was no risk that this would happen as regards a national sonship of God, and the high priest, being the servant and worshipper of the god, could not in any case be thought to be divine. But there *was* such a risk for Israel in the creation of a monarchy. It was not avoidable that the king of Israel should be termed Son of God, but the king was only son of God in an adoptive and counselling sense.

At the time of which we are writing the great danger to Israel lay in surrendering its own unique function as a priestly nation. The people came to the Prophet Samuel, and told him: "We *will* have a king over us, that we also may be like all the nations; and that our king may judge us, and go out before us, and fight our battles" (*I. Sam.* viii.19-20). And this was in spite of what Samuel had told them of how a king would be likely to act. With the Messianic concept of "a kingdom of priests" God alone had been king, and in this sense, in demanding a king, it was a rejection of God. (*I. Sam.* viii.7)

The circumstances radically endangered the Messianic Plan; but these might be overcome if there should be an ideal monarch who would receive the chrisma, the anointing. The first one to be chosen and anointed (christed) was Saul of the tribe of Benjamin. (*I. Sam.* ix)

Saul answered well enough, as it seemed, to what his people had demanded. He was physically tall and a competent commander. But, as time would show, there was a deep-seated weakness in him, which prevented him qualifying as an exemplary monarch. A dedicated king could indeed serve the Divine purpose, standing above divisions, and having at heart the best interests of all his people. The ideal royal Messiah could by precept and example inspire his people to implement their own Messianic function.

The ideal monarch is represented in retrospect in the following terms:

> When thou art come into the land which the Lord thy God giveth thee, and shalt possess it, and shall dwell therein, and shalt say, 'I will set a king over me, like as all the nations that are round about me'; thou shalt in any wise set him king over thee, whom the Lord thy God shall choose: one from among thy brethren shalt thou set king over thee: thou mayest not set a stranger over

thee, which is not thy brother. But he shall not multiply horses to himself, nor cause the people to return to Egypt... Neither shall he multiply wives to himself, that his heart turn not away: neither shall he greatly multiply to himself silver and gold.

And it shall be, when he sitteth upon the throne of his kingdom, that he shall write him a copy of this Law in a book out of that which is before the priests, the Levites: and it shall be with him, and he shall read therein all the days of his life; that he may learn to revere the Lord his God, to keep all the words of this Law and these statutes, to do them: that his heart be not lifted up above his brethren, and that he turn not aside from the commandments, to the right hand, or to the left: to the end that he may prolong his days in his kingdom, he, and his children, in the midst of Israel. (*Deut.*xvii.14-20)

We have a foreshadowing here of what would need to be the qualifications of Jesus if he was truly the Messianic king of Israel, including that he must be a Jew.

In close proximity to this description of the royal obligations there is a statement of the role of the prophet. God will not again speak directly, as at Sinai: he will communicate by means of prophets, who are to be tested by whether their predictions are verified. They will also serve as mentors of the monarch, and guides to the unfolding of the Messianic, so that there will continually be held before the nation its true purpose and destiny.

So now, ideally, Israel had a composite Messianic structure, consisting of high priest, king, and people, guided by the spirit of God manifesting through the prophets.

But let us continue here with the king.

Saul was superseded by David of Bethlehem. He was to answer in so many respects to the ideal king that there developed the belief that the ultimate royal Messiah would be one of his descendants. So we find in the *Psalms* that:

God chose David his servant, and took him from the sheepfolds: from following the ewes great with young he brought him to feed Jacob his people, and Israel his inheritance.
(*Ps.* lxxviii.70-71)

And again:
I have found David my servant; with my holy oil [the chrisma] have I anointed him: with whom my hand shall be established...

He shall cry unto me, 'Thou art my father, my God, and the rock of my salvation.' Also I will make him my firstborn, higher than the kings of the earth. My mercy will I keep for him for evermore, and my covenant shall stand fast with him. His seed also will I make to endure for ever, and his throne as the days of heaven. (*Ps.* lxxxix.20-29)

In another psalm God says:

I have anointed my king upon my holy hill of Zion. I will declare the decree: the Lord hath said unto me, 'Thou art my son; this day have I begotten thee' (*Ps.* ii. 6-7).

In some Gospel manuscripts these were the words Jesus heard when he was baptised in the Jordan.

This is the Messianic capacity, as God's chosen and anointed, *adopted* sonship of God was accorded to the people of Israel, to its monarchy, and to its priesthood (three categories). Christians with an ancestral paganism have neglected, or have been unwilling, to assimilate this, failing to apprehend that when sonship of God is ascribed to Jesus in the New Testament this was initially not in any supernatural sense, but in the Jewish Messianic sense, as the awaited chosen descendant of King David.

The promise was there from ancient times, and its fulfilment conveyed to the parents of Jesus before his birth. According to *Luke* his mother was told, "Thou shalt conceive in thy womb, and bring forth a son... He shall be great, and shall be *called* the son of the Highest: and the Lord God *shall give unto him the throne of his ancestor David*" (*Lk.* i. 31-32). This was no divine incarnation.

But we must return to the Hebrew monarchy. Following David, a brief period of glory ensued in the reign of Solomon the diplomat, the man of peace and wisdom. The great Temple was built at Jerusalem on Mount Zion with Phoenician skill and materials as the permanent home of the Ark of the Covenant. It seemed that Israel had achieved at least its own objective, of being a nation like all the other nations. But this, as we have seen, was not God's intention.

For nearly half a millennium the Hebrews experienced what was involved in statehood, as a buffer state between the powers of Egypt, Syria and Assyria, a battleground of competing sovereignties. In the event the kingdom became split between Israel and Judah. Israel was overrun and made captive. Judah endured for a time, but in her turn was conquered by the Babylonians.

In these centuries, for the most part, the Hebrew monarchs answered hardly at all to the ideal of kingship that was demanded. And as a consequence it seemed as if the mission entrusted to Israel had been no more than an idle dream, incapable of realisation. In vain did a succession of prophets give out their visions, and were persecuted for their pains.

There had been the experience of the prophet Elijah in the reign of Ahab and his queen Jezebel, when he had cried in despair to God, "because the children of Israel have forsaken thy covenant, thrown down thine altars, and slain thy prophets with the sword; and I, even I only, am left; and they seek my life, to take it away." And what does God answer? That there are still seven thousand in Israel, "all the knees that have not bowed unto Baal, and every mouth which hath not kissed him" (*I. Kings* xix. 10, 18).

Elijah was to find a prominent place in the Messianic Mystery as it would develop, as ultimate representative of the Priestly Messiah, whom Jesus believed had reincarnated as John the Baptist.

In the late priestly books of *Chronicles* there is a prayer put into the mouth of King Solomon anticipating the circumstances that were to arise, and from which it is desirable to quote the last section at some length.

> If they [thy people] sin against thee – for there is no man which sinneth not – and thou be angry with them, and deliver them over to their enemies, and they carry them away as captives unto a land far off or near; yet if they bethink themselves in the land whither they are carried captive, and turn and pray unto thee in the land of their captivity, saying, We have sinned, we have done amiss, and have dealt wickedly; if they return to thee with all their heart and with all their soul in the land of their captivity, whither they have carried them captives, and pray towards their land, which thou gavest unto their fathers, and towards the city which thou hast chosen, and towards the house which I have built for thy name: then hear thou from the heavens, even from thy dwelling place, their prayer and their supplications, and maintain their cause, and forgive thy people which have sinned against thee.
>
> Now, my God, let, I beseech thee, thine eyes be open, and let thine ears be attentive unto the prayer that is made in this place. Now, therefore, arise, O Lord God, unto thy resting place,

thou, and the Ark of thy strength: let thy priests, O Lord God, be clothed with salvation, and let thy saints rejoice in goodness. O Lord God, turn not away the face of thine anointed: remember the mercies of David thy servant. (*II. Chronicles* vi. 36-42)

# 4

# *Visions of the Ideal*

The centuries from Solomon to the Babylonian Exile were very significant, and we do well to study them closely. The human observer would be compelled to say that it was all nonsense to suppose that there could be any Divine Plan in view of its almost total rejection by those who were supposed to put it into operation. How in those circumstances could the Plan be valid, much less succeed?

There have been times – and this was one of them – when man with his limited vision could readily come to the wrong conclusion, crediting God with his own impatience and lack of resourcefulness. If this was God's Plan surely by now it would have succeeded. The fact of its abandonment by its participants in such a wholesale manner is proof enough that it was no more than a beautiful but idle dream. It is hard, even for the believer, to apprehend that God knows the End from the very Beginning, and that in having a Plan for our Planet all the contingencies that could arise have been taken into consideration.

In this instance we should take note of a new feature in the situation, the appearance of major prophets, who not only more graphically depicted the fruition of the Messianic programme, but also gave it a fresh emphasis. In the regal context there began to be depicted an ultimate personality as Messiah definitive.

This did not at all detract from the fruition of the other elements in the Messianic Plan, especially the basic part to be played by the Chosen People for the benefit of mankind. It provided a further assurance and guarantee of Israel's ultimate readiness to fulfil its function by reason of the exemplary faithfulness of a leader *par excellence*, who would exert a profound influence on his people.

The follies of the contemporary scene were challenged by visions of the ideal expressed in language which moves and inspires to this day. This is where the prophets came in, and we learn that "he that is now called a prophet was beforetime called a seer" (*I. Sam.* ix. 9).

Let us then recall some of the utterances of the pre-Exilic Hebrew prophets in relation to the ultimate fulfilment of Israel's mission, and in relation to the ideal king of Israel. We will begin with the Prophet Isaiah.

> And it shall come to pass in the last days, that the mountain of the Lord's house shall be established in the top of the mountains, and shall be exalted above the hills; and all the nations shall flow unto it. And many people shall go and say, 'Come ye, and let us go up to the mountain of the Lord, to the house of the God of Jacob; and he will teach us of his ways, and we will walk in his paths'; for out of Zion shall go forth the Law, and the Word of the Lord from Jerusalem. (*Isa.* ii. 2-3)

> The Lord will have mercy on Jacob, and will yet choose Israel, and set them in their own land: and the strangers shall be joined with them, and they shall cleave to the house of Jacob. (*Isa.* xiv. 1)

Regarding the Davidic Messiah we may cite the following passages from *Isaiah*, which are very well known, but which for the most part are not given their true meaning.

> Unto us a child is born, unto us a son is given: and the government shall be upon his shoulder: and his titles shall be proclaimed, 'Wonderful Counsellor, Mighty Hero, the Ever-living [lit. Father of Eternity], the Prince of Peace'. Of the increase of his government and peace there shall be no end, upon the throne of David, and upon his kingdom, to order it, and to establish it with judgment and with justice from henceforth even for ever. (*Isa.* ix. 6-7)

> There shall come forth a rod *out of the stem of Jesse*, and a branch shall grow out of his roots: and the spirit of the Lord shall rest upon him, the spirit of wisdom and understanding, the spirit of counsel and might, the spirit of knowledge and of the fear of the Lord; and he shall make him of quick understanding in the fear of the Lord: and he shall not judge after the sight of his eyes, neither reprove after the hearing of his ears... And righteousness shall be the girdle of his loins, and faithfulness the girdle of his reins. The wolf also shall dwell with the lamb, and

the leopard shall lie down with the kid... and a little child shall lead them... They shall not hurt nor destroy in all my holy mountain: for the Earth shall be full of the knowledge of the Lord, as the waters cover the sea. And in that day there shall be a root of Jesse, which shall stand for an ensign of the people; to it shall the Gentiles seek, and his rest shall be glorious. And it shall come to pass in that day, that the Lord shall set his hand again the second time to recover the remnant of his people... And he shall set up an ensign for the nations, and shall assemble the outcasts of Israel, and gather together the dispersed of Judah from the four corners of the Earth. (*Isa.* xi.1-12)

We move on to other prophets, quoting only a few pertinent passages.

The number of the children of Israel shall be as the sand of the sea... and it shall come to pass, that instead of it being said to them, 'Ye are not my people', it shall be said unto them, '*Ye are the sons of the living God*' (*Hos.* i.10).

The children of Israel shall abide many days without a king, and without a prince, and without a sacrifice... Afterwards shall the children of Israel return, and seek the Lord their God, and David their king; and shall fear the Lord and his goodness in the latter days. (*Hos.* iii. 4-5)

In that day will I raise up the tabernacle of David that is fallen... and I will raise up its ruins and I will build it as in the days of old... And I will bring again the captivity of Israel... And I will plant them upon their land, and they shall no more be pulled up out of their land which I have given them. (*Amos* ix.11-15)

Thou, Bethlehem Ephratah, though thou be little among the thousands of Judah, yet out of thee shall he come forth unto me that is to be ruler in Israel; whose goings forth have been foreseen from of old, from the days of eternity. (*Micah* v. 2)

Who is a God like unto thee, that pardoneth iniquity, and passeth over the transgression of the remnant of his heritage... He will turn again, he will have compassion upon us; he will subdue our iniquities; and thou wilt cast all their sins into the depths of the sea. Thou wilt perform the truth to Jacob, and the mercy to Abraham, which thou hast sworn unto our fathers from the days of old. (*Micah* vii.18-20)

Sing, O daughter of Zion; shout, O Israel; be glad and rejoice with all thy heart, O daughter of Jerusalem. The Lord hath taken away thy judgments... thou shalt not see evil any more... The Lord thy God in the midst of thee is mighty; he will save, he will rejoice over thee with joy... Behold, at that time I will undo all that afflict thee: I will save her that halteth, and gather her that was driven out; and I will get them praise and fame in every land where they have been put to shame. At that time will I bring you again, even in the time that I gather you: for I will make you a name and a praise among all people of the Earth, when I will turn back your captivity before your eyes, saith the Lord. (*Zeph.* iii.14-20).

Be glad then, ye children of Zion... Ye shall know that I am in the midst of Israel, and that I am the Lord your God, and none else: and my people shall never be ashamed. And it shall come to pass afterward, that I will pour out my spirit upon all flesh; and your sons and your daughters shall prophesy, your old men shall dream dreams, your young men shall see visions... And I will shew wonders in the heavens and in the earth, blood and fire, and pillars of smoke. The sun shall be turned into darkness, and the moon into blood, before the great and terrible day of the Lord come. But it shall come to pass, that whosoever shall call on the name of the Lord shall be delivered: for in Mount Zion and in Jerusalem shall be deliverance, as the Lord hath said... For, behold, in those days, and in that time, when I shall bring again the captivity of Judah and Jerusalem, I will also gather all nations, and I will bring them down into the valley of Jehoshaphat [i.e. 'the Lord is Judge'], and I will plead with them there for my people and for my heritage Israel, whom they have scattered among the nations, and parted my land. (*Joel* ii.23-iii.2)

The Lord also shall roar out of Zion, and shall utter his voice from Jerusalem; and the heavens and the earth shall shake; but the Lord will be the hope of his people, and the strength of the Children of Israel. So shall ye know that I am the Lord your God dwelling in Zion my holy mountain. Then shall Jerusalem be holy, and there shall no strangers pass through her any more... Judah shall abide for ever, and Jerusalem from generation to generation. (*Joel* iii.16-20)

We turn now to the major prophets Jeremiah and Ezekiel.

At that time they shall call Jerusalem the throne of the Lord; and all nations shall be gathered unto it, to the name of the Lord, to Jerusalem: neither shall they walk any more after the imagination of their evil heart. In those days the house of Judah shall walk with the house of Israel, and they shall come together... to the land I have given for an inheritance unto your fathers. (*Jer.* iii.17-18)

I will gather the remnant of my flock out of all the countries whither I have driven them, and will bring them again to their folds... Behold, the days come, saith the Lord, when I will raise unto David a righteous branch, and a king shall reign and prosper, and shall execute judgment and justice in the earth. (*Jer.* xxiii.3-8)

Alas! for that day is great, so that none is like it: it is even the time of Jacob's trouble; but he shall be saved out of it. For it shall come to pass in that day, saith the Lord of hosts, that I will break his yoke from off thy neck, and will burst thy bonds, and strangers shall no more serve themselves of him; but they shall serve the Lord their God, and David their king, whom I will raise up unto them. (*Jer.* xxx.7-9)

Behold, I will bring them from the north country, and gather them from the coasts of the earth... They shall come with weeping, and with supplications will I lead them... for *I am a father to Israel, and Ephraim is my firstborn*. Hear the word of the Lord, O ye nations, and declare it in the isles afar off, and say, 'He that scattered Israel will gather him, and keep him as a shepherd does his flock' (*Jer.* xxxi.8-10).

Behold, the days come, saith the Lord, that I will sow the house of Israel, and the house of Judah, with the seed of man, and with the seed of beast. And it shall come to pass, that like as I have watched over them, to pluck up, and to break down, and to throw down, and to destroy, and to afflict; so will I watch over them, to build, and to plant, saith the Lord... Behold, the days come, saith the Lord, that I will make a new covenant with the house of Israel, and with the house of Judah: not according to the covenant that I made with their fathers... which my covenant they break... But this shall be the covenant that I will make with the house of Israel: after those days, saith the Lord, I will put my Law in their inward parts, and write it in their hearts; and I will be their God, and they shall be my people. (*Jer.* xxxi. 27-33)

Behold, I will gather them out of all countries, whither I have driven them in mine anger... and I will bring them again unto this place, and I will cause them to dwell safely: and they shall be my people, and I will be their God... And I will make an *everlasting* covenant with them, that I will not turn away from them... Yea, I will rejoice over them to do them good, and I will plant them in this land assuredly with my whole heart and with my own soul. For thus saith the Lord; 'Like as I have brought all this evil upon this people, so will I bring upon them all the good that I have promised them' (*Jer.* xxxii. 37-42).

In those days, and at that time, will I cause the branch of righteousness to grow up unto David; and he shall execute judgment and righteousness in the land. In those days shall Judah be saved, and Jerusalem shall dwell safely... For thus saith the Lord: 'David shall never want a man to sit upon the throne of the house of Israel; neither shall the priests, the Levites, want a man before me... to do sacrifice continually.' Thus saith the Lord: 'If my covenant be not with day and night, and if I have not appointed the ordinances of heaven and earth; then will I cast away the seed of Jacob... so that I will not take any of his seed to be rulers over the seed of Abraham, Isaac and Jacob...' (*Jer.* xxxiii.15-26).

In mine holy mountain, in the mountain of the height of Israel, saith the Lord God, there shall all the house of Israel... serve me: there will I accept them, and there will I require your offerings, and the firstfruits of your oblations, with all your holy things. I will accept you... when I bring you out from the people, and gather you out of the countries wherein ye have been scattered; and I will be sanctified in you before the heathen. (*Ezek.* xx. 40-41)

Prophesy therefore concerning the land of Israel, and say unto the mountains, and to the hills, to the rivers, and to the valleys, Thus saith the Lord God: 'Behold I have spoken in my jealousy and in my fury, because ye have borne the shame of the heathen.' Therefore thus saith the Lord God: 'I have lifted up mine hand. Surely the heathen that are about you, they shall bear their shame. But ye, O mountains of Israel, ye shall shoot forth your branches, and yield your fruit to my people of Israel; for they are at hand to come. For, behold I am for you, and I will turn unto you, and ye shall be tilled and sown: and I will multiply men upon you, all the house of Israel, even all of it: and the cities shall be inhabited, and the wastes shall be builded...' (*Ezek.* xxxvi.6-10).

I will take you from among the heathen, and gather you out of all countries, and will bring you into your own land. Then will I sprinkle clean water upon you, and ye shall be clean... A new heart also will I give you, and a new spirit will I put within you... and cause you to walk in my statutes, and ye shall keep my judgments, and do them. And ye shall dwell in the land that I gave to your fathers; and ye shall be my people, and I will be your God. (*Ezek.* xxxvi.24-28)

Then he said unto me, Son of Man, these bones are the whole house of Israel: behold, they say, 'Our bones are dried up, and our hope is lost: for we are cut off for our parts.' Therefore prophesy and say unto them, Thus saith the Lord God: Behold, O my people, I will open your graves, and cause you to come up out of your graves, and bring you into the land of Israel. And ye shall know that I am the Lord, when I have opened your graves... And I will make them one nation in the land upon the mountains of Israel; and one king shall be king to them all... David my servant shall be king over them; and they all shall have one shepherd: they shall also walk in my judgments, and observe my statutes, and do them. And they shall dwell in the land that I have given unto Jacob my servant... They shall dwell therein, even they, and their children, and their children's children for ever: and my servant David shall be their prince for ever. (*Ezek.* xxxvii.11-25)

And he said unto me, 'Son of Man, here is the place of my throne, and the place of the soles of my feet, where I will dwell in the midst of the children of Israel for ever, and my holy name shall the house of Israel no more defile...' (*Ezek.* xliii.7).

These are only a few brief extracts from the Prophets, but they are remarkably clear and consistent, visualising a Golden Age when the people of Israel, finally restored to their land, shall have become "a kingdom of priests and a holy nation" under the example and guidance of an ideal ruler of the house of David. It is in the context of this destiny that sonship of God is applied to both the Messianic nation and its leader, in a symbolic not in a pagan literal sense. Israel also is the people of the New Covenant as well as of the Old. There is no, so to speak, swapping horses in midstream. If Christians have a claim on the New Covenant it can only be as members of the house of Israel, observing the laws governing Israel. And who, in the Christian view, is the eternal David of the Prophetic vision? Jesus believed that it was himself.

It is important to do what I have done here, providing what is called a *catena*, similar to those which were put together in relation to Jesus, and even by Jesus himself (*Lk*. xxiv. 27), to confirm that he was the predicted Messiah. What Christians call the Old Testament was the Bible of Jesus and his immediate followers. They must read it in the same way and to the same effect, without dodging the implications. That is why I have italicised certain words.

# 5

# *Thus Spake Zarathustra*

The Babylonian Exile followed by the Return when the Babylonians were conquered by the Persians, had a profound influence on the development of Messianic thinking. The Jews found themselves in close contact with civilizations which had advanced ideas of astronomy and astrology, with views of the interplay between the heavenly and the earthly. The heavens became a more populous region in which a variety of forces were operative, and there was a continuous battle in progress between the powers of Good and Evil. Ultimately, of course, the Good would triumph.

As a consequence it came to be more positively recognised by the Jews that the destiny of Israel was bound up with a Divine programme, which progressively was working itself out. There was no blind fate, but an intelligent correspondence between the intentions of God and the world of human affairs. And with that correspondence there went the concept of 'As above, so below'. The factors on Earth had a counterpart in the skies, involved in the plan that was to bring Heaven on Earth. Each individual, and even each nation, had an angelic counterpart. There was even a Jerusalem Above. *Genesis* was now interpreted so that Adam had been made in the likeness of the Archetypal Man in Heaven, and in process of time the Jewish mystics would identify that man (the Son of Man) with the earthly Messiah's heavenly counterpart.

However, the immediate effect of the Return was not one of exaltation or exultation. There was now a deep sense of contrition for the unfaithfulness of the past, and a more comprehensive determination to become a Holy Nation in fact, a desire to be taken back into service, which would be performed more diligently, more conscientiously.

There was also the conviction that by its sufferings Israel was not only paying a price for its own transgressions, but also expiating the sin of the world. It is here that we meet with the Suffering Servant of the Second Isaiah in association with Israel's return to Zion. The sufferer is the Jewish people, not a particular individual identified with Jesus as Messiah. We must take *Isa.* liii in conjunction with the chapters which immediately precede it. "Listen, O isles, unto me; and hearken, ye people from afar; the Lord hath called me from the womb; from the bowels of my mother hath he made mention of my name… And he said unto me, 'Thou art my servant, O Israel, in whom I will be glorified…'" (*Isa.* xlix.1, 3).

"And he said, 'It is a light thing that thou shouldest be my servant to raise up the tribes of Jacob… I will also give thee for a light to the Gentiles, that thou mayest be my salvation unto the ends of the earth'" (*Isa.* xlix.6).

Restored from captivity the new Israel would grow up before God "as a tender plant, and as a root out of a dry ground: he hath no form nor comeliness; and when we shall see him, there is no beauty that we should desire him. He is despised and rejected of men, a man of sorrows, and acquainted with grief… Surely he hath borne our griefs, and carried our sorrows: yet we did esteem him stricken, smitten of God and afflicted. But he was wounded for our transgressions, he was bruised for our iniquities: the chastisement of our peace was upon him: and with his stripes we are healed…" (*Isa.* liii.2-5).

Out of the misery and the suffering there must come home to every Jew the consciousness of the nation's unique vocation from which there could be no escape. The legend of the Prophet Jonah was created, the man who had tried to run away from his duty to preach repentance to the great city of Nineveh, but had been brought back to it after virtual extinction.

The Messianic figures of the new beginning were Joshua the high priest and Zerubbabel the prince 'the son of oil' (*Zech.*iv). They would head the rebirth and the reconstruction which would result in the conversion of many heathen. "And many nations shall be joined to the Lord in that day, and shall be my people: and I will dwell in the midst of thee… And the Lord shall inherit Judah his portion in the Holy Land, and shall choose Jerusalem again" (*Zech.* ii.11-12).

Thus the return from Babylon gave promise of a new era, and once more the seers directed their vision to an ultimate ideal to encourage and inspire their contemporaries.

The Prophet Haggai is told: "Speak now to Zerubbabel the son of Shealtiel, governor of Judah, and to Joshua the son of Josedech, the high priest, and to the residue of the people, saying, 'Who is left among you that saw this house [the Temple] in her first glory? And how do you see it now? In comparison, is it not in your eyes as nothing? Yet now be strong... For thus saith the Lord of hosts: Yet once, it is a little while, and I will shake the heavens, and the earth, and the sea and the dry land... and I will fill this house with glory... The glory of this latter house shall be greater than of the former, saith the Lord of hosts: and in this place will I give peace'" (*Haggai* ii. 2-9).

"Thus saith the Lord of hosts: 'Behold, I will save my people from the east country, and from the west country; and I will bring them, and they shall dwell in the midst of Jerusalem: and they shall be my people, and I will be their God, in truth and in righteousness...' Thus saith the Lord of hosts: 'It shall yet come to pass, that there shall come people, and the inhabitants of many cities... saying, Let us go speedily to pray before the Lord, and to seek the Lord of hosts: I will go also... In those days it shall come to pass, that ten men shall take hold – out of all languages of the nations – even shall take hold of the skirt of him that is a Jew, saying, We will go with you: for we have heard that God is with you'" (*Zech*. viii. 7-23).

"Remember ye the Law of Moses my servant, which I commanded unto him in Horeb for all Israel, with the statutes and judgements. Behold, I will send you Elijah the Prophet before the coming of the great and dreadful Day of the Lord: and he shall turn the heart of the fathers to the children, and the heart of the children to their fathers, lest I come and smite the earth with a curse" (*Mal*. iv. 4-6).

After the promise of good things it is on this sombre warning note that the word of the Prophets closes. The Messianic is not going to succeed just by waiting for it to happen; but only by the total commitment of Israel to its function.

We can see here how a new note was being struck after the return from exile. There was being reflected in the prophetic writings a much greater sense of Israel's world mission, its corporate responsibility for the salvation of all mankind, so that there would be a universal turning of the nations towards the One God, and thus towards Israel as his representative. Only thus could the destiny of the Earth be completed, with all mankind brought into peace and fellowship, and thus to fitness for a still wider service in the universe. While there

34

needed to be a personal Messiah for Israel, there needed to be a nation-Messiah for all nations.

Thus the idea of a Divine Plan now took hold more positively as an outcome of the Babylonian and Persian experiences. The Plan would progress over a succession of Ages towards an ultimate goal. Pious mystics in Israel found it agreeable to the Messianic process that it should reflect a contest between the forces of Good and Evil, as conceived by the Persians. Apart from everything else this would explain why so often in Israel's story the People of God had been enticed and led astray. The Evil Power could be responsible, seeking in this way to impede and frustrate the accomplishment of God's purposes. It seemed reasonable that there could be a high spiritual force, Satan and Belial, as antagonist, in one aspect tempting and testing the righteous, and in another jealous of the Divine sovereignty, and lusting after personal aggrandisement.

So just as in each day Light and Darkness succeeded each other, so in the story of the Ages should there be alternations, as Good and Evil strove for the mastery. But Jewish faith would never allow that the force of Evil could be on a par with the Good, and would never allow that it could rate higher than a fallen angel and his minions. However challenged, God as the only deity must be unique and supreme. There had therefore to be conceived on God's side a heavenly champion of the Good at a lower level of being.

This was not difficult to imagine once it had been accepted that there were correspondences between what was Above with what was Below, as we have noted. There would then be conceived also a third dimension, a lower realm than the surface of the Earth, a Tartarus, Hell or Gehenna, a place of flame and agony for the disobedient, whether angels or men.

It took several centuries for such concepts to develop among Jewish mystics, and only in a very crude form did they reach the people in general. They could accept to an elementary extent the idea of the heavenly counterpart, and of an age-old warfare between the Children of Light and the Children of Darkness. They could also accept the notion of a commerce between Heaven and Earth in the heathen manner, so that heavenly beings could appear on Earth, and humans could be taken to Heaven if they were of exceptional merit. There impressed itself the idea of a succession of Ages, moving towards a climax for the world, which would see the fruition of human concepts of a Plan of God which was working itself out, and recognise the

35

choice that was given to every individual to be on the side of Good or Evil.

What did not register with the Jews was that the Earth was somewhere from which to escape, that the material was essentially evil. The Earth was man's home, where with God's help he must make his own heaven. Here the Messianic hope served as a vital corrective of human disgust with death and corruption. It insisted on a process of redemption, whereby ultimately sin and death and all corruption would be abolished. By a bodily change from mortality to immortality our world would become a Paradise Regained.

In this respect Judaism showed itself to be more responsive to a Divine objective in placing man on this planet, and of a purpose of God in history. The Prophetic illumination prevailed that there had been a Divine motivation behind the Creation, behind the Call of Abraham, behind the Sojourning in Egypt, behind the Testing in the Wilderness, behind the Bitterness of the Exile, which would justify the selection of the People of Israel, and which would have its fruition in the Latter Days.

The world would be full of the knowledge of God as the waters cover the sea. The goal of human aspiration would have been reached, and this would be seen to justify the Ways of God with Man, and the travail of God's People.

But the Jewish sages did gain a great deal from the heady contact with the Orient, and later with the Occident. From the former they accepted in large measure that the outcome of the story had been known from the beginning, that it was all written in the stars. From the latter they acknowledged that the universe was ruled by wisdom and not by chance.

However, what was wise need not necessarily be fair, and what was predestined need not necessarily be just. The Jews, therefore, maintained their insistence that "the God of all the Earth must do right". All that happened must in the end be shown to be perfectly just. There could be no two ways about this, no veering to the right or to the left. If God was not a God of absolute justice he did not qualify to be God at all. The Jews might be condemned as being excessively legalistic; but for them the Torah (the Law) was the evidence that God was to be loved because he could be trusted absolutely, always and only, to do what was right and fair, as a child should expect of his father.

# 6

# *A Kingdom of Priests*

Until near the middle of the second century BC popular Jewish thinking had tended to concentrate on the Messianic in the regal sense, the advent of the ideal king of the house of David. In spite of the pronouncement that Israel would be to God "a kingdom of priests and a holy nation" the priestly Messianic aspect had remained secondary. But now circumstances would arise which would bring it into prominence.

A new era for the Jews had begun with the meteoric career of Alexander of Macedon in the second half of the fourth century. According to the Jewish records Alexander had been most favourable to the Jewish faith, and conferred many favours on the Jews. He would give them a substantial part of his new city of Alexandria in Egypt, and a number of Jews accompanied his army in its victorious campaigns. As a consequence of Alexander's patronage Greek culture became all the rage, and eventually in Egypt around the middle of the second century BC the Hebrew Bible appeared in a Greek version (the Septuagint). Already in Alexander's time Greek culture began to make its impact, and there was the great attraction of his One World outlook. Many were now willing to abandon their Judaism and accommodate themselves to the new and enticing universalism. The doctrine of the Holy Nation and its mission, so very demanding in its requirements, began to seem outdated and no longer valid. Why should there be this restrictive separatism?

It was going to take a great shock and much suffering to get the Jews back on course, as it had done at other times and would do again in the future. It was not for Israel to join the nations, to become Gentilized, but rather to evangelise them. This was the significance of the Biblical book of *Jonah*. Somehow a force always came into operation to prevent Israel's merger with the rest of mankind. The phenomenon would receive the not very appropriate name of anti-semitism. Enemies would arise to seek to root out the Jews and extinguish them, forcing them back into isolation.

But this aim to destroy Israel could never be accomplished, however grievous the assault, for the Messianic mission for which Israel was selected must be fulfilled, not for Israel's sake, but for the sake of all mankind. Eventually the Messianic priestly identity of Israel would have to be accepted by Israel.

The blows did not begin to fall until around two hundred years after Alexander, when the land of Israel was under the Syrian Seleucid rulers. The circumstances were signalled about 170 BC. I have related them in a book I wrote in 1956 (*Secrets of the Dead Sea Scrolls*), from which I may take some extracts.

At this time Jesus son of the High Priest Simon II supplanted his brother Onias III, and taking the name of Jason went over to the Greek way of life. 'And thus,' says the author of *II. Maccabees* (iv.13), 'there was an extreme of Greek fashions, and an advance of an alien faith, by reason of the exceeding profaneness of Jason, that ungodly man and no high priest.' Regarding the same apostasy the writer of *I. Maccabees* (i.11-15) states: 'In those days there came forth out of Israel transgressors of the Law, and persuaded many, saying, "Let us go and make a covenant with the Gentiles that are round about us; for since we were parted from them many evils have befallen us." And the saying was good in their eyes. And certain of the people were forward herein and went to the king, and he gave them licence to do after the ordinances of the Gentiles. And they built a place of exercise in Jerusalem; and they made themselves uncircumcised, and forsook the holy covenant, and joined themselves to the Gentiles, and sold themselves to do evil.'

We can follow the course of events not only in the *Apocrypha*, but in several ancient documents, such as the *Assumption of Moses*. Things were to go from bad to worse, reaching a climax in the reign of Antiochus Epiphanes. Those loyal to God were subjected to a tortured death.

But the persecution of those who refused to apostasise also had a salutary effect. It called into being a body of the faithful, known as Chasidim (the Pious), a number of whom belonged to the priesthood. A new readiness, a new determination manifested itself to become much more strict in devotion to the ideal of a Holy Nation, a Priestly People.

Among the loyalists were some who described themselves as Sons of Zadok, who had been high priest in the time of David. We have learned much more about them from their writings which have been recovered, commonly known as the Dead Sea Scrolls. They had a leader in one known as the Teacher of Righteousness, a priestly figure of Messianic stature who believed there must be a new Exodus for the faithful, a new sojourn in the wilderness, the making of a New Covenant, which would isolate the Righteous Remnant from contamination. The main body of them emigrated and formed a colony in the region of Damascus in Syria. In their expectation a Priestly Messiah would be of more consequence than the Royal Messiah, acting as his mentor and guide, so that he should not depart from God's Law. Eventually the Zadokites would give rise to the Essenes and Therapeuts with a widespread organization on which the followers of Jesus would lean, but also having an inner identity as the repository of many secrets of interpretation of the Scriptures, employing various codes, and knowledge of healing arts, which they claimed had been handed down from Shem the son of Noah.

I would refer the reader who would know more to the book of mine mentioned, and to a more recent one of mine, *The Essene Odyssey*.

The persecutions were bound to have their reactions. And while the apostasising of the second century BC owed much to power-seeking high priests, the reassertion of faithfulness to God and his Law was also to come from the priesthood. It was the priest Mattathias, with his five sons, who started a resistance movement. "He saw the blasphemies that were committed on Judah and Jerusalem, and he said, 'Woe is me! Wherefore was I born to see the destruction of my people... and behold, our holy things and our beauty and our glory are laid waste, and the Gentiles have profaned them'" (*I. Macc*. ii.6, 12).

One of the sons, Judas Maccabaeus, raised the standard of revolt against the Syrians. "Then were gathered together unto them a company of Chasidim, mighty men of Israel, every one that offered himself willingly for the Law (i.e. of Moses). And all they that fled from the evils were added to them, and became a stay to them. And they mustered a host" (*I. Macc*. ii.42-43). The arch-enemy of Judas was the apostate high priest Alcimus, and it has been proposed that the mysterious Teacher of Righteousness had been one who had denounced him, as also the distinguished Chasid Joseph son of Joezer. Judas was to have his triumph when Jerusalem was liberated and the

Temple cleansed, but subsequently he was to die in battle. He was succeeded by his brother Jonathan, who was involved in the rivalries between Syria and Egypt. Israel was to know no peace for many years. Finally a measure of independence was secured under John Hyrcanus, son of Simon Maccabaeus. He died in 104 BC.

With John Hyrcanus there was a new development of the Messianic mystery, for with him the regal status was subordinated to the priestly. He was a priest upon his throne, exercising sovereignty, but at the same time acting as civil ruler, and he was credited with the power of prophecy. For a period the hope of a Davidic Messiah not only took second place but almost slipped out of sight. With John in mind, the author of the *Testaments of the Twelve Patriarchs* visualises the ultimate era.

> And in the seventh week shall come priests [who are] idolaters, adulterers, lovers of money, proud, lawless, lascivious, abusers of children and beasts. And after their punishment shall have come from the Lord, the priesthood shall fail. Then shall the Lord raise up a new priest. And to him all the words of the Lord shall be revealed; and he shall execute a righteous judgment upon the earth for a multitude of days. And his star shall arise in heaven as of a king, lighting up the light of knowledge as the sun the day. And he shall be magnified in the world. He shall shine forth as the sun on the earth, and shall remove all darkness from under heaven, and there shall be peace in all the earth. The heavens shall exult in his days, and the earth shall be glad...
> The heavens shall be opened, and from the temple of glory shall come upon him sanctification, with the Father's voice as from Abraham to Isaac. And the glory of the Most High shall be uttered over him, and the spirit of understanding and sanctification shall rest upon him. For he shall give the majesty of the Lord to his sons in truth for ever more; and there shall none succeed him for all generations for ever. And in his priesthood the Gentiles shall be multiplied in knowledge upon the earth, and enlightened through the grace of the Lord. In his priesthood shall sin come to an end, and the lawless shall cease to do evil...
> (*Test. XII Patriarchs, Levi* xvii.11-xviii.9).

This glowing picture of a Priestly Messiah reflected the initial idealism of the Sadducean Party in Israel. There were now two major parties in Israel, the Sadducees and Pharisees. Under the Hasmonean rulers the former represented an aristocracy as the party of government. The Pharisees prided themselves on representing democracy, as the Jewish people's party. They were not priests, but priestly after a fashion, in so far as they emphasised the old ideal of a sacerdotal nation. They were the founders of the Synagogue where the people could be taught their function, and they interpreted the Torah (the Law of Moses) by spelling out its provisions in a particularist manner, their applications virtually constituting a second Torah, even more strict, safeguarding the first.

The Pharisees accepted that there should be a priestly Messiah; but in their view a Royal Messiah, coming from the laity, should be paramount, for it was the people as a whole which was to be inspired by his example, and thus perform in the world the function of the People of God. In the end they opted for a prophetic and priestly personality as the Royal Messiah's forerunner. It was written that in the Last Days the Prophet Elijah would return. The Pharisees claimed that Elijah had also been a priest.

These conflicting views, as we shall see, would be a cause of conflict between the followers of John the Baptist and of Jesus. The former insisted that John was the Messiah, while for the latter Jesus had been supreme, combining in himself the functions of both king and priest.

But meanwhile another Messianic personality was being conceived by the mystics, who had his origin in the figure of the Patriarch Joseph the son of Jacob.

# 7

# *A Joseph Messiah*

It is a curious fact of Messianic lore that the name Joseph should come into prominence in the immediate pre-Christian period of Jewish history. It is away from the mainstream anticipations of the Priestly and Royal Messiahs from the tribes of Levi and Judah. This Messianic figure answers to the experiences of another of the sons of Jacob, Joseph. He would be cut off from his brothers, and lost to them, yet ultimately he would be the means of their salvation.

In the persecutions of the Seleucid period many sages and saints had lost their lives, or had been driven into exile like the Teacher of Righteousness. The new Joseph cult seemed to be a means of claiming that their sufferings had not been in vain, and that they had been performing an atoning work for their people. In the *Book of Jubilees* we even have the suggestion that the annual feast day, the Day of Atonement, had been instituted with reference to the Patriarch Joseph.

> And the sons of Jacob slaughtered a kid, and dipped the coat of Joseph in the blood, and sent it to Jacob their father on the tenth of the seventh month... For this reason it is ordained for the Children of Israel that they should afflict themselves on the tenth of the seventh month – on the day that the news which made him weep for Joseph came to Jacob his father – that they should make atonement for themselves with a young goat on the tenth of the seventh month, once a year, for their sins. (xxxiv.12-18)

In an earlier book of mine I had noted that in the Seleucid period a famous Chasid and priest named Joseph son of Joezer had suffered martyrdom for his faith. He had been an opponent of the Wicked Priest Alcimus. I had also observed that the persecution of the Essene Teacher of Righteousness by the Wicked Priest was linked with the Day of Atonement in the *Commentary on the Prophet Habakkuk* in the Dead Sea Scrolls.

Regarding the Patriarch Joseph, he is further introduced to us as a Messianic type in the *Testaments of the Twelve Patriarchs* (*Test. Benjamin*). The text has manuscript variations, and we have also to allow for changes and interpretations made in this work by Christian scribes, so that the predictions in them would relate to Jesus, who significantly had a Joseph as his father.

Do ye also, therefore, my children, love the Lord God of heaven and earth, and keep his commandments, following the example of the holy and good man Joseph. For until his death he was not willing to tell regarding himself; but Jacob, having learnt it from the Lord, told it to him. Nevertheless he kept denying it. And then with difficulty he was persuaded by the adjurations of Israel (i.e. Jacob). For Joseph also besought our father that he would pray for his brethren, that the Lord would not impute to them as sin whatever evil they had done unto him. And thus Jacob cried out: 'My good child, thou hast prevailed over the bowels of thy father Jacob.' And he embraced and kissed him for two hours, saying, 'In thee shall be fulfilled the prophecy of Heaven, which says that the blameless one shall be defiled for lawless men, and the sinless one shall die for godless men.'

Christians unfamiliar with immediately pre-Christian Jewish apocalyptic literature will not be aware to what lengths the Church would go to claim fulfilments in Jesus of predictions in such documents. In this passage we not only have language applicable to the Crucifixion, but also to *Lk.* xxiii.34, "Father, forgive them; for they know not what they do."

So now, for the groups of the ultra-pious in Israel, there was coming into prominence a new Messianic personality, the Martyr Messiah or Son of Joseph Messiah, whose function was to suffer on behalf of his people.

Fundamentally, the Martyr Messiah represented the Faithful in Israel, who believed that their sufferings were performing an atoning work for Israel. Many of these, like the Teacher of Righteousness and his followers, were undergoing the Joseph experience of persecution and exile, the latter largely self-imposed. They banished themselves to the Land of Damascus, and there is a curious passage about this in the *Damascus Rule*.

When the two houses of Israel separated, all who proved faithless were delivered to the sword, and those who held fast (i.e. to the

43

Covenant) escaped to the Land of the North. *As He said, 'And I will cause to go into captivity Siccuth your king and Chiun your images, the star of your god which ye made for yourselves, beyond Damascus'* (*Amos* v.26-27). The books of the Law are the tabernacle of the king, as He said, (*Amos* ix.11) *'And I will raise up the tabernacle of David that is fallen'* (cf. *Acts* xv.16). 'The king' is the congregation, and 'Chiun your images' are the books of the Prophets, whose words Israel has despised. And 'the star' is he who studied the Law, who came to Damascus, as it is written, *'There shall come forth a star out of Jacob, and a sceptre shall rise out of Israel'* (*Num.* xxiv.17). 'The sceptre' is the prince of the congregation (*Damascus Rule* VII).

The star of *Numbers* xxiv is interpreted not as coming forth in the sense of arising in Israel, but as emigrating (going forth) from Israel.

The third Messianic personality, the Suffering-Servant or Martyr Messiah, inevitably found its inspired source in the fifty-third chapter of the post-exilic Deutero-Isaiah, which was to count for so much in the convictions of Jesus.

Initially the Suffering-Servant represented those in Israel who had maintained their devotion to God at the cost of their lives; but they are depicted in the singular, and in a manner which is extremely moving. The language, especially in the antique English, is both beautiful and emotional. We need quote here only certain parts of the text.

He is despised and rejected of men; a man of sorrows, and acquainted with grief: and we hid as it were our faces from him...

Surely he hath borne our griefs, and carried our sorrows: yet we did esteem him stricken, smitten of God and afflicted. But he was wounded for our transgressions, he was bruised for our iniquities...

All we like sheep have gone astray; we have turned every one to his own way; and the Lord hath laid on him the iniquities of us all... He is brought as a lamb to the slaughter, and as a sheep before her shearers is dumb, so he openeth not his mouth.

He was taken from prison and from judgment... for he was cut off out of the land of the living: for the transgression of my people was he stricken.

And he made his grave with the wicked, and with the rich in his death; because he had done no violence, neither was any deceit in his mouth ... He shall see of the travail of his soul, and shall be satisfied: for by his knowledge shall my righteous servant justify many; for he shall bear their iniquities.

Therefore will I divide him a portion with the great ... because he hath poured out his soul unto death: and he was numbered with the transgressors; and he bare the sin of many, and made intercession for the transgressors.

We have here a vision of the Christ-Collective, the residuary faithful in Israel which would perform an atoning work for the whole nation, suffering in the process antagonism and persecution. But it lent itself to application in an individual sense at a later time, adding an extra dimension to the concept of the Messianic.

Another exchange of the individual for the collective would be made with the figure of the Son of Man (i.e. a human being as other than a beast). In the late book of *Daniel* the Son of Man represents ideal Israel which is to supersede a succession of Brute kingdoms (vii), the first like a lion, the second like a bear, the third like a leopard, the fourth, the most terrible of all, unlike any other beast. These have been interpreted to relate to Babylon, Persia, Greece and Rome, the succession of militant imperialisms. In the time of the last of these kingdoms God would set up a kingdom of another order which would never be destroyed. This would be the kingdom of the Saints of the Most High.

But the Jewish mystics were to take the Son of Man in a personal rather than a collective sense in their Messianic scheme. This is brought out in the *Enoch* literature. Man (according to *Genesis)* had been made in the image of God. That image must therefore be represented in heaven by a manlike figure, earthly man's spiritual counterpart, Adam Kadmon, original Adam. In *Enoch* this primeval and heavenly Son of Man is equated with the Messiah.

Since the *Enoch* literature will be unfamiliar to many of my readers I will need to quote from it at some length.

And there [in heaven] I saw One who had a head of days [i.e. the Ancient of Days], and his head was white like wool, and with him was another being whose countenance had the appearance of a man and his face was full of graciousness like one of the holy angels. And I asked the angel who went with me and showed me all the hidden things, concerning that Son of Man, who he was, and whence he was, and why he went with the Head of Days. And he answered and said unto me, 'This is the Son of Man who hath righteousness, and who reveals all the treasures of that which is hidden, because the Lord of Spirits hath chosen him, and his lot before the Lord of Spirits hath surpassed everything in uprightness for ever. And this Son of Man whom thou hast seen will arouse the kings and mighty ones from their couches and the strong from their thrones. And he will put down the kings from their thrones and kingdoms because they do not extol and praise him, nor thankfully acknowledge when the kingdom was bestowed upon them. (*Enoch*, Sect. II, xlvi.1-5, tr. Charles)

And at that hour the Son of Man was named in the presence of the Lord of Spirits and his name before the Head of Days... He will be a staff to the righteous on which they will support themselves and not fall, and he will be the light of the Gentiles and the hope of those who are troubled of heart. All who dwell on earth will fall down and bow the knee before him and will bless and laud and celebrate with song the Lord of Spirits. And for this reason has he been chosen and hidden before him before the creation of the world and for evermore. And the wisdom of the Lord of Spirits hath revealed him to the holy and righteous... because they have hated and despised this world of unrighteousness... And in those days the kings of the earth, and the strong who possess the earth, will be of downcast countenance... And I will give them over into the hands of mine elect: as straw in fire and as lead in water they will burn before the face of the holy... And on the day of their affliction, there will be no one to take them with his hands and raise them: for they have denied the Lord of Spirits and his Anointed. (xlviii.1-10)

And in those days will the earth also give back those who are treasured within it... And he [i.e. God] will choose the righteous and holy from among them: for the day of their redemption has drawn nigh. And the Elect One will in those days sit on my throne, and all the secrets of wisdom will stream forth from the counsels of his mouth: for the Lord of Spirits hath given it to him and hath glorified him... Their faces [i.e. of the Elect] will be lighted up with joy because in those days the Elect One has appeared, and the earth will rejoice and the righteous will dwell upon it, and the elect will go to and fro upon it. (li.1-5)

And the Lord of Spirits seated him [i.e. the Messiah] on the throne of his glory and the spirit of righteousness was poured out upon him, and the word of his mouth slew all the sinners, and all the unrighteous were destroyed before his face... And the kings and the mighty and all who possess the earth will glorify and bless and extol him who rules over all, who was hidden. For the Son of Man was hidden before him [i.e. God] and the Most High preserved him in the presence of his might and revealed him to the elect... And the righteous and elect will be saved on that day and will never again from thenceforth see the faces of the sinners and unrighteous. And the Lord of Spirits will abide over them, and with that Son of Man will they eat and lie down and rise up for ever and ever. (lxii.2-14)

The reader familiar with the Gospels will readily recognize echoes of this teaching in the parables related by Jesus in *Matthew* xxv, where it is made very clear that the ultimate home of the righteous will be a redeemed earth over which the Messiah will reign in his second advent.

Jesus was to describe himself as the Son of Man in the sense of the book of *Enoch*, and he and his Jewish followers believed that he became the Messiah at his baptism, when the heavenly Son of Man descended upon him and entered into him. This was the reason why he was driven into the wilderness to be tempted by Satan in his new capacity. The pagan doctrine of the Trinity was not conceived until very much later, and could never have been entertained by Jesus himself.

It should now begin to be appreciated that by the middle of the first century BC there was no single commonly expressed doctrine of the Messiah. There were versions both individual and collective, priestly and regal, mystical and political. Some of these we shall need to explore further, to correct commonly held misconceptions, especially by orthodox Christians.

# 8

# *Complexities*

At the dawn of the Christian Era the Messianic Hope among the Jews had become much more intense and diversified. This is not apparent to the Christian who bases himself on the New Testament, which he regards as an inspired authority. He is not aware that the Gospels are propaganda documents in which the narratives have been subordinated to the view that Jesus was uniquely the Christ, and only his expression of the Messianic was the true one. Being composed for converted Gentiles they go even further in varying degrees, to identify being the Messiah with a status of deity as Son of God in a contemporary pagan sense. Inevitably they have given rise to false interpretations and the perversion of history. And though there is a considerable amount of historical material available, this is twisted or ignored by most Christian scholars, and not revealed at all to the man-in-the-pew.

Accordingly, it is commonly represented that Jesus was a man of peace, and that the Jews rejected and made away with him because they were awaiting a Warrior Messiah. Even worse is the slander that the Jews crucified Jesus as a blasphemer because he claimed deity. This arose because of the necessity to identify the Messianic with Deity for the benefit of Gentiles, for whom it was alien and peculiarly related to the Jewish People.

We shall have need, therefore, to rewrite the story of Christian Beginnings at some length, first in relation to the Messianic complexities of the period, and second in relation to the followers of Jesus in Israel whose teaching came from Jesus and those who had been closest to him. In doing this we will need to furnish information which hardly any Christians are aware of because it has been suppressed, and relate the ideas to the historical circumstances with which they are bound up.

We may begin with the point that the Jews were awaiting a Warrior Messiah. It is completely wrong to refer to 'the Jews' in a general sense. As we have partly seen, there were current various imaginations of the Messiah among the Jewish people, differing greatly from one another in the presentation of sects and parties. The idea of a Warrior Messiah was mainly favoured by the common people and extreme nationalists due to the pro-Roman ruler Herod the Great and his oppressive measures which had turned Israel into a police state. This had been followed by the direct Roman rule of Judea after the deposition of Herod's successor Archelaus. The Messianic in a militant sense was the natural expectation of the Resistance Movement, and had nothing to do with the interpretation of Scripture.

When we come to bodies with a Biblical background like the Pharisees, the position was very different. We have a record of the kind of Messiah they were expecting, which I must quote at some length since many of my readers will never have encountered it.

> Behold, O Lord, and raise up unto them their king, the son of David, in the time which thou, O Lord, knowest, that he may reign over Israel thy servant; and gird him with strength that he may break in pieces them that rule unjustly. Purge Jerusalem from the heathen that trample her down to destroy her, with wisdom and with righteousness.
>
> He shall thrust out the sinners from the inheritance, utterly destroy the proud spirit of the sinners, and as potter's vessels with a rod of iron shall he break in pieces all their substance. He shall destroy the ungodly nations with the word of his mouth, so that at his rebuke the nations may flee before him, and he shall convict the sinners in the thoughts of their hearts.
>
> And he shall gather together a holy people, whom he shall lead in righteousness; and shall judge the tribes of the people that hath been sanctified by the Lord his God. And he shall not suffer iniquity to lodge in their midst; and none that knoweth wickedness shall dwell with them. For he shall take knowledge of them, that they be all the sons of their God, and shall divide them upon the earth according to their tribes. And the sojourner and the stranger shall dwell with them no more. He shall judge the nations and the peoples with the wisdom of his righteousness. Selah.
>
> And he shall possess the nations of the heathen to serve him beneath his yoke; and he shall glorify the Lord in a place to be

seen of the whole earth; and he shall purge Jerusalem and make it holy, even as it was in the days of old. So that the nations may come from the ends of the earth to see his glory, bringing as gifts her sons that had fainted, and may see the glory of the Lord, wherewith God hath glorified her.

And a righteous king and taught of God is he that reigneth over them; and there shall be no iniquity in his days in their midst, for all shall be holy and their king is the Lord Messiah [or, Lord's Anointed]. For he shall not put his trust in horse and rider and bow, nor shall he multiply unto himself gold and silver for war, nor by ships shall he gather confidence for the day of battle. The Lord himself is his King, and the hope of him that is strong in the hope of God.

And he shall have mercy upon all the nations that come before him in fear. For he shall smite the earth with the word of his mouth even for evermore. He shall bless the people of the Lord with wisdom and gladness.

He himself also is pure from sin, so that he may rule a mighty people, and rebuke princes and overthrow sinners by the might of his word. And he shall not faint all his days, because he leaneth upon his God; for God shall cause him to be mighty through the spirit of holiness, and wise through the counsel of understanding, with might and righteousness. (*Psalms of Solomon* XVII. 23-42)

Here we have an application of the vision of the Messiah in *Isaiah* xi. It is "with the rod of his *mouth*" that he smites the earth, and "with the breath of his *lips*" that he slays the wicked, not with weapons of war.

If we compare the words of Jesus reflected in *Matthew* and *Mark* we shall appreciate that his understanding of his mission and function as Messiah was identical with that of the author of the *Psalms of Solomon*. There is brought out what we have earlier disclosed from the Prophets, that the Messiah's responsibility in his regal aspect was exclusively to his people Israel, to bring them back to an appreciation of *their* responsibility as the nation-Messiah for the nations, "a kingdom of priests, and a holy nation". Ultimately, of course, all nations will come under Messiah's government in the era of the establishment on earth of the Kingdom of God.

But while the view of the Pharisees was the dominant one, there were the Essenes and some of the Sadducees who concentrated on the Priestly Messiah, the second Messianic personality. He would be of the priestly tribe of Levi, as the regal one would be of the tribe of Judah. As we saw in Chapter 6, hopes had been entertained that the priestly ruler John Hyrcanus would prove to be the Priestly Messiah. Now, at the beginning of the Christian Era, another priestly figure suddenly appeared on the scene to qualify as the Priestly Messiah. This extraordinary personality was John the Baptist.

Christians are not aware of the Christ-status of John the Baptist, because in the New Testament everything is done to suppress it. But even today, in the Middle East, there are those who still believe it.

As far back as 1929 I wrote a book (*The Lost Book of the Nativity of John*, T. & T. Clark, Edinburgh) dealing with the Birth Legends of the Baptist in his Messianic capacity, and I must now resurrect some of the evidence.

The policy of the Gospel writers, crystallized in the saying put into the mouth of the Baptist in the Fourth Gospel, "He [Jesus] must increase but I must decrease," was consistently directed to utilizing this historic figure as the supreme witness to the Messiahship of Jesus, and then, his purpose served, to relegate him to the position of Prophetic Forerunner (Elijah redivivus). Indeed, he is made specifically to deny that he is the Christ (*John* i.20). But in Christian records there has also survived glimpses of a higher role assigned to the Baptist by many. In *Luke* we find that "the people were in suspense, and all men debated in their hearts of John, whether he were the Christ or not" (iii.15).

The Church Fathers were well aware that there were still those who favoured John's Messiahship. The *Clementine Homilies*, speaking of the Jewish sects, remarks: "Yea, some even of the disciples of John, who seemed to be great ones, have separated themselves from the people, and proclaimed their own master as the Christ" (xxiii).

The Nativity stories relating to John the Baptist told of his birth in Bethlehem, his father being the priest Zechariah and his mother Elizabeth. The Magi from the East had informed King Herod that Bethlehem would be the place of the Messiah's birth. When news of this reached Elizabeth she fled with her son to the wilderness to a place of concealment, and he could not be found. John's father Zechariah was interrogated in the Temple by Herod's officers, but claimed that he did not know where his son was. This version of the story is preserved in the *Book of James*. The text then states:

And Herod was enraged, and said: 'His son is destined to be

king over Israel.' And he sent to Zechariah again, saying, 'Tell the truth; where is thy son? For thou knowest that thy life is in my hands.' So Zechariah was murdered in the Temple, and John remained in the wilderness until the time of his appearance to Israel.

Another version, however, claims that John, as the infant Messiah, was removed from his parents by his guardian angel, and kept in concealment until he was grown up. Only then, at the age of twenty-two, was he brought back to Jerusalem and reunited with his parents in their extreme old age (*Sidra d'Yahya*). This is the version of the Mandaeans of the Lower Euphrates recovered by the late Lady Drower. What John had believed about himself, the evidences do not permit us to ascertain. But it is clear that he was of priestly stock, and therefore could qualify as the Priestly Messiah. His sudden appearance in Israel, wearing the garb of one of the prophets of old, proclaiming the near advent of the Kingdom of God on earth, and dipping the people in the Jordan in token of repentance, can be accepted as historical fact. We can also accept that Jesus was profoundly impressed and inspired by John's ministry, and went to him for baptism.

John's activities, like those of Jesus, were directed to the same end, the recovery, through repentance, of the people of Israel as the Nation-Messiah, through which the nations of the world (the Gentiles) would come to know the One God, and thus create on Earth the Kingdom of God.

Certainly, at the dawn of the Christian Era, there was a sudden outpouring of a prophetic and apocalyptic literature, and spiritual and political upheavals in Israel, which testified to the contemporary conviction that the climax of the ages was being reached.

A problem was certainly created by uncertainty as to whether Jesus could be the Messiah, since his family resided in Galilee and most of his public activities were conducted in Galilee. In *John* we read of a dispute on this matter in Jerusalem (*John* vii. 41-42), because, according to the Prophet Micah, the Davidic Messiah would be born in Bethlehem in Judea (*Micah* v.2).

The issue was regarded as of such consequence, and especially as John the Baptist had been born in Bethlehem, that evidence was called for that Jesus too had been born there. *Matthew* and *Luke* both set out to do this, and their stories are completely contradictory.

*Matthew* states positively that Jesus was born in Bethlehem in the reign of King Herod (d. 4 BC). We then have the account of the visit of the Magi to Bethlehem, and of Herod's design to kill the infant Messiah. His father, warned of this by an angel, escapes with the child and his mother to Egypt, and they remain there until Herod's death. Herod was succeeded by his son Archelaus, so Joseph was afraid to return to Judea, and settled in Nazareth in Galilee.

*Luke* furnishes a totally different version. Joseph and Mary are inhabitants of Galilee, residing at Nazareth. Mary has a relation in Judea, Elizabeth the wife of the priest Zechariah. *Luke* is careful not to say that Elizabeth lived at Bethlehem. It just says "a city of Judah". The infant in Elizabeth's womb, the future John the Baptist, pays homage to the future mother of the Messiah. Later, when Mary is in an advanced state of pregnancy, she and Joseph travel to Bethlehem because of a decree by the Roman Emperor Augustus instituting a tax, which required that all subjects should go for registration to their ancestral home. This taxation, it is said, was first made when Cyrenius [Quirinius] was Roman governor of the province of Syria.

There is no reference to this taxation by the Jewish historian Josephus who lived in the first century AD who states (*Jewish Antiquities*, Bk. XVIII) that the census was carried out by Quirinius when Archelaus, successor to Herod, had been deposed by the Romans, and Judea had been annexed to the Roman province of Syria. This was in AD 6-7, while of course Herod had died in 4 BC. Ramsay tried hard to claim that Quirinius had also been governor of Syria prior to 4 BC, but in any case the Romans had no jurisdiction over Judea in Herod's lifetime. The census business was just a device of Luke to bring Joseph and Mary from Galilee to Bethlehem, so that Jesus would be born there. The probabilities are that Jesus was by birth a Galilean.

So controversial was the issue of the regal and priestly Messiahs represented by Jesus and John the Baptist that the supporters of Jesus found it necessary (as in the *Epistle to the Hebrews*) to claim that Jesus had in fact been a priest, not Levitic but of the order of Melchisedek (*Ps.* cx.4), who was both king of Salem [Jerusalem] and priest of the Most High God (*Gen.* xiv.18) Actually, it was claimed of the brother of Jesus, who succeeded him as leader of the Nazoreans, that he had officiated in the Temple as High Priest (Epiphanius, *Panarion*, lxiii; see also Eusebius' *Ecclesiastical History*, II.xxiii). The Maccabaean priest-kings had also employed for themselves the title of 'Priest of the Most High God'.

53

Because of *Luke's* statement that the mothers of Jesus and John the Baptist were related, the possibility presented itself that Mary was of Levitic rather than Judean descent. This view is attacked by Ephraim the Syrian in his *Gospel Commentaries*, as I pointed out in my book on the *Nativity of John*, from which I may quote.

> "But if," Ephraim says, "because the Scripture said, 'Elizabeth thy sister,' you therefore think that this was said that it might be made manifest that Mary was of the house of Levi, in another passage the same Scripture said that they were both, Joseph and Mary, of the house of David."

Elsewhere, strangely enough, St. Ephraim himself speaks of Jesus as a Levite. When Jesus sent Peter to catch a fish in order to pay the tribute money, the Pharisees went with him. "And when he had drawn out the fish, which had in its mouth a stater, the symbol of dominion, those haughty ones were reproved and confounded, because they believed not that he was a Levite, to whom the sea and the fishes were witnesses that he is king and priest." In one version of the text of John's Gospel, *Codex Algerinae Peckover*, this reading is found in connection with this incident (*doceat se mare, me non solum sacerdotem esse, sed et regem*).

Nowadays, the Messianic is so far removed from Christian concern that, at least among laymen, matters of this sort are seldom if ever discussed. Yet for Jesus his Messianic status was paramount, and if he did not qualify as Messiah there was no point in his manifesting himself in Israel, or at this juncture in history when Messianic expectation was rife.

# 9

# *The Time Has Come*

Jesus and John the Baptist shared the same conviction, "The time has come, and the Kingdom of God is at hand." From the literature of the period we can confirm that this conviction was widespread, which was the reason why Messianic personalities should now appear in Israel.

In those days there was no consciousness of any hiatus, so that the Messiah would manifest himself at this time, but his reign from Zion as world ruler was not to be expected for many centuries. Jesus, having studied the predictions, and being no more than human, believed the same as other Jewish seers of his period. Consequently there were many keeping a look-out for the Signs of the Times. Jesus chided his audience with being so busy watching out for the Signs that they could not see what was under their noses. Instead of watching for Signs they should have been repenting as the people of Nineveh had repented at the preaching of Jonah. Later it was conveyed by Christians that the Sign of Jonah was a reference to the resurrection of Jesus, because Jonah had been three days and nights in the belly of the great fish which had swallowed him.

Even the Jewish historian Josephus in the first century, writing as he was for non-Jews, dwells on the Signs of the end of the Era, and claimed the Messiahship for the Roman general Vespasian, who had been proclaimed emperor on Jewish soil.

It is important to appreciate what kind of circumstances were being looked for in the political sphere by the Jewish seers as evidence of the advent of the Messiah and the inauguration of his government. The expectation was that the Messiah would come to a troubled world, full of wars and rumours of wars, a world of tyrants and tribulation, and especially there would come into prominence an iron kingdom, the fourth beast of the prophecies of *Daniel* (vii) "dreadful and terrible, and strong exceedingly, and it had great iron teeth: it devoured and brake in pieces, and stamped the residue with its feet."

The kind of tyrant that was looked for was seen in the person of Herod the Great, while the Fourth Beast was readily identified as Imperial Rome. Consequently in the first century AD it was to be anticipated that in the days of those kings the God of heaven would set up a kingdom which would never be destroyed, the Son of Man kingdom. "And the kingdom and dominion, and the greatness of the kingdom under the whole heaven, shall be given to the people of the saints of the Most High" (*Dan.* vii. 27).

We learn much of the reign of Herod in the pages of Josephus, as I have set down elsewhere (*The Passover Plot*, ch. I). With real and imagined plots against him, he could not feel secure until he had destroyed the Hasmoneans, around whom popular support could still gather. First to be got rid of was Antigonus, then the boy Aristobulus whom he had made high priest at the age of sixteen, and then the aged former high priest and king, the inoffensive Hyrcanus II. Later the Hasmonean princess Mariamne, whom he had married and genuinely loved, was executed, followed by her mother Alexandra, and to the end of his days the king's fear of conspiracy by family and friends led him on even to the destruction of his own children. His subjects hated and feared him, and were kept from revolt only by the strongly-manned fortresses which Herod constructed at strategic points and by his conversion of the country into what we would now call a police state.

To quote Josephus directly: "At this time (c. 20 BC) Herod remitted to the people of his kingdom a third part of their taxes... For the more important purpose of getting back the goodwill of those who were disaffected. For they resented his carrying out such arrangements as seemed to them to mean the dissolution of their religion and the disappearance of their customs... Herod, however, gave a most careful attention to this situation, taking away any opportunity they might have [for agitation] and instructed them to apply themselves at all times to their work. No meetings of citizens were permitted, nor were walking together or being together permitted, and all their movements were observed. Those who were caught were punished severely, and many were taken, either openly or secretly, to the fortress of Hyrcania, and there put to death. Both in the city and on the open roads there were men who spied upon those who met together" (*Antiq.* XV.365-366).

Herod is said to have shown leniency to the Essenes, possibly because when he was a young man they had foretold that he would become king. His rule was regarded as one of the Signs of the Times, and reflected in a prophetic book dating from early in the first century AD. We read there: "An insolent king [Herod] will succeed them [the Hasmoneans], who will not be of the race of the priests, a man bold and shameless, and he will judge them [the people] as they deserve. And he will cut off their chief men with the sword, and will destroy them in secret places, so that no one may know where their bodies are. He will slay the old and the young, and he will not spare. Then the fear of him will be bitter unto them in their land. And he will execute judgments on them as the Egyptians executed upon them, during thirty and four years, and he will punish them" (*Assumption of Moses*, vi.2-6).

How many Christians at Christmas are informed that this was the state of affairs in Israel at the time that John the Baptist and Jesus were born?

It was almost immediately after Herod's death that the Romans came on the scene, since Herod had appointed Caesar Augustus as executor of his will. Herod's son Archelaus had travelled to Rome to secure the endorsement of the emperor of his succession after a Jewish rising against him at the Passover of 4 BC when some three thousand were killed. Anticipating trouble, Quinctilius Varus, Roman legate of Syria, had placed a legion at Jerusalem. Trouble did break out at the feast of Pentecost with an attack on the Roman forces. Multitudes were slain, and in the course of the struggle the Romans set fire to the porticoes of the Temple and plundered its treasury. The revolt spread to other parts of the country, forcing Varus with his troops and Arab allies to take prompt action. Two thousand of the Jewish rebels were crucified.

An echo of the event is found in a parable attributed to Jesus of "a certain nobleman [who] went into a far country to receive for himself a kingdom, and to return... But his citizens hated him, and sent a message after him, saying, 'We will not have this man to reign over us.' And it came to pass, that when he was returned, having received the kingdom... [he said,] 'Those mine enemies, which would not that I should reign over them, bring hither, and slay them before me'" (*Lk*. xix.12-27).

In the event Archelaus did not obtain Herod's throne. Caesar made him ethnarch in the south of Israel, while other parts of the country were to be governed by two other sons of Herod, Philip and Herod Antipas. Archelaus, however, seemed to have learnt nothing about how he should rule his subjects, and in AD 6 the Romans deposed him. His kingdom was converted into an administrative region, consisting of Judea, Samaria and Idumea, under a Roman procurator responsible to the Roman legate of the province of Syria, at this time Quirinius.

Thus Zion now came under the rule of the heathen 'the iron kingdom', and became liable to the Roman census for taxation instituted by Quirinius in 6 AD.

At this time, according to the *Assumption of Moses* (vii), "the times will be ended," and therefore the Last Times would begin. Everything seemed to be pointing to be approaching climax of the ages.

It was in freedom-loving Galilee that the resistance movement found ready support. Here Judas son of Hezekiah raised the banner of liberty from the pagan yoke with the slogan "No Ruler but God", while in the south a certain Simon claimed the kingship, and was killed by the Romans. The extremist party of the Zealots was born, and the Old Russian version of Josephus claims that John the Baptist first appeared at this time, and was one of them. "He came to the Jews and summoned them to freedom, saying, 'God hath sent me to show you the Way of the Law, whereby you may free yourselves from many masters; and there shall be no mortal ruling over you, but only the Highest, who has sent me.'" The passage follows II.110 of the *Jewish War*, and it is consistent with the recovered Essene *Manual of Discipline*, where it is declared:

> And when these things shall come to pass to the Community of Israel, in these determined moments they shall separate themselves from the midst of the habitation of perverse men, to take to the wilderness to prepare the Way of Him as was written; 'Prepare ye in the wilderness the Way of the Lord: make straight in the desert a highway for our God' (*Isa.* xl.3). This Way is the study of the Law... so as to act according to all that was revealed time after time, and according to what the Prophets revealed by his Holy Spirit.

It is to be noted that at least one of the twelve chosen by Jesus as his representatives was a Zealot. The circumstances were evidently much grimmer than has generally been supposed. An End-Time obsession had been created, giving rise to a national hysteria. "Such (writes Josephus) was the great madness that settled upon the nation because they had no king of their own to restrain the populace by his pre-eminence, and because the foreigners who came among them to suppress the rebellion were themselves a cause of provocation through their arrogance and their greed" (*Antiq.* XVII.277).

From this time Imperial Rome, whose ruler claimed Sonship of God, was clearly indicated as the Antichrist, the last Great power to be the challenger of the Messiah, and therefore to be abolished by him when he inaugurated his kingdom.

As we shall disclose, the early Christians were therefore antagonistic to Imperial Rome, and this was the true reason why the Romans persecuted them. It had nothing to do with a new religion. The Christians were persecuted for doing things "contrary to the decrees of Caesar, saying that there is another king, one Jesus" (*Acts* xvii.7).

Long before this the Jewish propagandists had been interpolating the *Sibylline Oracles*, prized and venerated in the Mediterranean world; and the Christians would contribute their quota. Several of these *Oracles* were directed against Rome. We may give one or two instances.

> But when Rome shall rule over Egypt, though still delaying, then shall the great kingdom of the Immortal King [i.e. the Kingdom of God] appear among men, and a holy king [i.e. the Messiah] shall come who shall rule over the whole earth for all ages of the course of time. Then shall implacable wrath fall upon the men of Latium... and all men shall perish beneath their own roof-tree, when the torrent of fire shall flow down from heaven. Ah, wretched me, when shall that day come, and the judgment of immortal God, the great King? Yet still be ye builded, ye cities, and all adorned with temples and theatres, with market squares and images of gold, silver and stone, that so ye may come to the day of bitterness. For it shall come, when the smell of brimstone shall pass upon all men. (Bk. III.45-60)

> But then there shall be the beginning of another empire from the western sea [i.e. Rome], white and many-headed which shall rule over wide lands, and overthrow many, and make all kings to fear thereafter, and ravish much gold and silver out of many cities... And in those days there shall be great tribulation among men, and it shall bring all to confusion and disorder, filling the world with evils... Then shall the people of the great

59

God once more be strong, they who are to be the guides of life to all mankind. (175-195)

The Christian oracles would make an even more positive attack on the Roman Empire comparable to the book of *Revelation* in the New Testament. We can learn much more from these records about the actual anticipations of the early Church of the climax of history and the Second Advent than we can from the New Testament itself. And the picture is very different and much more harsh than what Christians wish it to be believed.

What we have just now established is that Rome's intrusion into the Holy Land at the dawn of the first Christian century was taken to be evidential of the climax of history, calling for the Messiah to manifest himself, followed by the circumstances which would usher in the Kingdom of God on earth.

# 10

# *In Search of Jesus*

The convictions regarding the Last Times were bound to produce the response of claimants of the Messiahship. Outstanding among them were John the Baptist and Jesus, respectively representing the Priestly Messiah and the Davidic Messiah. The more popular expectation was that of the king of Israel, and from what we can learn about Jesus he understood the requirements of that office better than any who at various times would lay claim to it. The existence of Christianity for almost two thousand years bears testimony, however distorted, to the conviction engendered by his powerful personality and compre-hension.

But how may we make contact with the Jesus of history rather than the divine being of pagan Christian imagination? There has been much quest for the historical Jesus; but largely this has been impeded by the assumptions of the Christian Faith. Jesus was a Jew of Israel, and our quest for him must centre primarily on evidences relating to his own homeland. Here the canonical Gospels, composed in other lands and having to resort to the fictional amplification of some genuine traditions, have to be treated as of secondary service. Between them and the events of the time of Jesus is the great hiatus caused by the Jewish war with the Romans which ended with the fall of Jerusalem in AD 70.

However, we do have in the letters of the Envoy Paul evidence that belongs to the intermediate period. As regards Paul himself he is not a good witness, in so far as he had never companied with Jesus and was not concerned to report on what he had said and done. For him Jesus was the Messiah, at present abiding in Heaven, but shortly to return to Earth to inaugurate his kingdom.

The reason for Paul's reticence was that, unlike the immediate Envoys of Jesus, he had had no association with Jesus when he was on Earth, and was thus at a disadvantage compared with the Twelve. This was a sore point, especially as those converted to belief in Jesus by him could turn from him to members of the Twelve as better informed than he was about the views of Jesus. There were controversial issues involved, relating to the obligations of converts from the Gentiles to become practising Israelites since Jesus was king of Israel.

Paul insists in a letter to the Christians at Corinth that he does not have to uphold his commendation of himself to them, just because he had not companied with Jesus. Everything was new now. So even if he had known Christ in the flesh that no longer mattered. "Therefore if any man is in Christ, he is a new creature: old things are passed away; behold, all things are become new" (*II. Cor.* v. 17).

The very fact that Paul clashed with the Twelve over the question of whether converted Gentiles must be subject to the Law of Moses tells us several things. The first is that adherence to Jesus as Messiah had not involved for his immediate disciples any change in religion. They remained practising Jews. Therefore Jesus himself must have set an example in his loyalty to Judaism. Indeed, unless he did so, he could not have claimed to be the Messiah, since this was one of the Messiah's paramount functions.

Among the Twelve was Simon Peter (Cephas) who had been particularly close to Jesus, and had become travelling Envoy to the Jews of the Diaspora (*Gal.* ii. 7). He came to Antioch, where a Christian community had been formed as a result of Paul's work, and in his enthusiasm treated the converts from the Gentiles as if they were full Jews, and had no hesitation in eating with them. But when emissaries arrived from James, the brother of Jesus, Peter ceased doing this. This incident is related from Paul's viewpoint in his letter to the Galatians. (*Gal.* ii. 9-16)

But what Paul in his bitterness neglected to emphasize was that for him too Gentiles who had accepted Jesus as Messiah had ceased to be Gentiles, and consequently Peter was not so much to blame. The persons in question were now fellow-citizens. Peter, in an extant letter to converts from the Gentiles, would write:

> But ye are a chosen generation, a royal priesthood, an holy nation, a peculiar people [i.e. identical with Israel]; that ye should shew forth the praises of him who hath called you out of darkness into his marvellous light: which in time past were not a

people, but are now the people of God, which had not obtained mercy, but now have obtained mercy. (*I. Pet.* ii. 9-10)

Accordingly they are to have their conversation honest among *the Gentiles* (as being no longer such), "that, whereas they speak against you as evildoers, they may by your good works, which they behold, glorify God in the Day of Visitation" (*I. Pet.* ii. 12).

We must be very careful, therefore, not to fall into the trap of supposing that the issue between Paul and Jerusalem was whether Gentiles should come under the Law in order to be saved, but whether they were entitled to be regarded as Israelites if they did not come under the Law incumbent on Israel. We shall return to this question later on.

We have now learnt, however, to be very confident that Jesus was a real person, a pious Jew who believed himself to be the awaited Messiah. However reluctant Paul was to speak of the activities of Jesus, in which he had not personally participated, he could not avoid testifying to some things incidentally. Jesus was survived by intimates who remained loyal to him and were loyal Jews, and who had made their headquarters in Jerusalem.

But we learn more from Paul. He knows nothing about a Virgin Birth. Jesus had been born a Jew in a normal manner (*Gal.* iv. 4). He was a descendant of King David (*Rom.* i. 3). His activities were testified to not only by his disciples, who remained faithful to him, believing that after his crucifixion he had been raised from the dead and taken to Heaven from whence he would shortly return to establish the Kingdom of God; they were supported by members of his family. (*I. Cor.* ix. 5).

It is of very great consequence that at the head of all the followers of Jesus was his younger brother, next in age, James (Jacob). He was someone known to history, and we are able to learn a great deal about him, as will be shown in due course. But we must not underestimate the significance of the fact that the closest followers (the Twelve) and nearest relations of Jesus (his brothers) were so convinced of his Messiahship that they were prepared to travel far and wide and endure every kind of hardship to proclaim their conviction.

Paul mentions the appearances of Jesus after his resurrection, which he had been told about (*I. Cor.* xv. 5-8). One of these was to his brother James. It is not mentioned in any of the canonical Gospels, but it was related in the *Gospel of the Hebrews* in a passage that has been preserved. It is conveyed by Jerome, *Of Illustrious Men*, that in the Hebrew Gospel it was recorded that James the brother of Jesus had sworn that he would fast until he had seen Jesus risen from the dead. Jesus did appear to him, and taking up bread he blessed and broke it and gave it to James, saying, "My brother, eat thy bread, for the Son of Man is risen from them that sleep."

James, in fact, was to become someone in the nature of Prince Regent pending his exalted brother's return, and titular head of all persons in all lands who owned Jesus as King-Messiah. Associated with him in the government of the communities were Peter and John. The latter was not John the son of Zebedee, but John the Priest, author of the *Book of Revelation*. As mentioned above, the head-quarters of the Movement was at Jerusalem, and from the descriptions provided by the *Acts of the Apostles* we can now see, since the recovery of the Dead Sea Scrolls, that its organization was derived from that of the Essenes, whose principal period of report and assembly was the Jewish festival of Pentecost. Paul himself was bound by the regulations, and had to report on his activities to the Council at Jerusalem. On one occasion he would not stay longer at Ephesus because he had to get to Jerusalem by Pentecost (*Acts* xviii.21).

The last time Paul went to Jerusalem to report to James and the Elders of the Nazoreans, as the followers of Jesus were known, they told him, according to the *Acts* (xxi.20): "Thou seest, brother, how many *myriads* [i.e. tens of thousands] of Jews there are which believe [in the Messiahship of Jesus], and they are all zealous of the Law." This is a very startling statement, as is another (Acts vi.7) that a great number of Jewish priests gave their allegiance to Jesus. Within a very few years of the death of Jesus vast multitudes of faithful practising Jews (not converts to any new religion) were owning Jesus as their awaited Messiah. This is a tremendous testimony to the impact he had made, and to his own personal loyalty to the religion of Israel. Had Jesus abandoned Judaism, or if he had made the claims about himself embodied in the Church's Creeds, nothing like this could have happened. It should be clear to any honest and open-minded inquirer that a Gentilised Church, antisemitic in character, wilfully falsified the truth, and it is high time that erudite Christian theologians acknowledged this.

What other evidences do we have from before the Jewish war with the Romans in AD 66-70 that point to a knowledge of Jesus? Here we depend very much on Christian sources no longer available but quoted by various Church Fathers.

It would seem that there was a moment in time when the decision was taken by the intimates of Jesus to carry word of him as Messiah to all the Jews of the Diaspora. We learn of a tradition that Jesus had told the apostles not to leave Jerusalem for twelve years (Eusebius, *The History of the Church* V. xviii). This is supported by Clement of Alexandria, quoting the lost *Preaching of Peter*, where Jesus had said, "If any one of Israel will repent, to believe in God through my name, his sins shall be forgiven him. After twelve years go forth into the world, that no one may say, 'We have not heard'" (*Stromateis*, VI.vi). The date would be approximately AD 48.

The circumstances would have called for common propaganda material as evidence of the Messiahship of Jesus. Tradition points to the creation of two brief documents, whose compilation is linked with the name of Matthew. One of these was a collection of passages from the Old Testament relating, it was believed, to the Messiah, and how these had been fulfilled in the experiences of Jesus. The *Gospel of Matthew* furnishes some of the passages, and an amplified version of them was used by Justin Martyr in his *Dialogue with the Jew Trypho*. The other document quoted things which Jesus had said and done, especially his teaching. This was a Jewish practice, reporting the words of famous rabbis. By these means a certain amount of reliable material would become available to subsequent Gospel writers, which they could work up and amplify to suit their own requirements for the benefit of non-Jewish Christians.

In documents of this kind there would inevitably be a good deal of propaganda material colouring the circumstances and the sayings, and they would be enlarged and altered to an appreciable extent for the benefit of non-Jews as time went on. So we need to be cautious about such evidences. Rather more helpful is what underlies the *Gospel of Mark*, if the tradition is correct that it largely reflects the personal reminiscences of Peter in his speeches to Christian groups.

We learn from Papias via Eusebius (*The History of the Church*, iii.39) that he had been informed that "Mark, having become the interpreter of Peter, wrote down accurately everything that he remembered, without however recording in order what was said or done by Christ."

This is a valuable statement. Mark's Gospel uniquely brings us in contact not so much with evidences of the Messiahship of Jesus as with his public activities, mainly in Galilee, as recalled by one of his closest associates. Peter had spoken of what he remembered to Gentile Christians in a personal capacity, in addition to the propaganda line employed in common by all apostles. He employed his native Galilean Aramaic, and Mark acted as his interpreter, taking notes of his statements. Later, however, when Mark wished to incorporate this material in a book, he was handicapped by his own notes which had not recorded precisely what sayings of Jesus had been associated with which incidents. Mark, of course, was writing for non-Jewish believers, which possibly may account for the explanation of Jewish customs and words.

It is clear from what has been called the Synoptic tradition that his Gospel was of great service to the authors of *Matthew* and *Luke*, who felt that they could rely on it.

In face of these evidences it would be a very foolish person who wished to argue that Jesus had never existed. Of course the story would progressively be altered and amplified for propaganda reasons, both for Jews and Gentiles, and in the interests of a new theology and an increasing antisemitism. But much may still be found in the Gospels by those concerned with history by comparing some statements and allusions with the evidences of non-Christian sources. Jesus emerges as very much a man of his time, and still more a devout Jew of his time, dedicated in a Messianic capacity to his people's world mission.

# 11

# *Jesus Found*

The two important facts about Jesus, which the canonical Gospels do not dispute, are that he was a member of the Jewish race and faith and that he believed himself to be the Messiah (Christ) his people were eagerly awaiting. It stands to reason, therefore, that anyone wishing to discover and comprehend him must familiarize himself with Jewish beliefs and convictions to which he subscribed. For Christians in general, including the most erudite, this is extremely difficult because of their own religious traditions and convictions. They cannot readily escape from being Gentiles in outlook with their roots in ancient paganism. It does not, therefore, suffice for them that Jesus should be a Jewish Messiah, a status peculiar to the ideas of his own people. He must also, and more importantly, be something else, of consequence in a Gentile context. It has been one of the great problems of Christianity as it developed that while it was both Jewish and Pagan it was neither Jewish nor Pagan. The attempt to unite two incompatible positions would produce the doctrine of the Trinity and the imagination that Jesus could be at one and the same time both God and Man.

In the first century of the Christian Era there would be no problem in holding that Jesus was king of the Jews. And in that capacity it would be natural for Gentiles to regard him as Son of God, since this was the status of contemporary rulers, some of whom would take it very literally. In the Roman empire it had been adopted by Augustus, who authorised the building of temples in which he was worshipped. A typical inscription, dated 7 BC, hailed him as "Caesar, who reigns over the seas and continents, Jupiter, who holds from Jupiter his father the title of Liberator, Master of Europe and Asia, Star of all Greece, who lifts himself up with the glory of great Jupiter, Saviour."

But this idea of a ruler elevated to the rank of Son of God was not the same thing as an incarnation. It was also believed that the gods could appear on earth in human likeness, which also was not actual incarnation. In the *Acts of the Apostles* Paul and Barnabas were credited respectively at Lystra with being Jupiter and Mercury wearing human appearance (*Acts* xiv.11-12). Even for Jews an angel could manifest himself to men in this manner. Wearing the likeness of a man was not what became attributed to Jesus by the Gentile Church: it was that he was *very* God and *very* man, simultaneously completely divine. In this way it was held that Jesus was much more than a Messiah, while seeking to safeguard that there was only One God.

The theory was to create difficulties for many Christians, notably those described as Docetists, who insisted that if Jesus was really divine he could only have worn the appearance of a man, since human flesh was both sinful and perishable. As divine he could not therefore have suffered on the cross and died, since an immortal must be deathless. Some would conceive that someone was made by God to look like Jesus and suffered on the cross instead of him. The Docetists were not dropping the deity of Jesus: they were dropping his humanity. Both could not possibly be true. They had sense on their side, even if it was the wrong side.

Jesus, as Messiah, as the king of Israel, was entitled to refer to himself as son of God in the Jewish adoptionist sense which did not imply deity. The people of Israel too was so described, as we have seen. Customarily, as the Gospels show, Jesus described himself as the Son of Man, a title which only had a Messianic significance for Jewish mystics (*John* xii.34). This tells us a great deal about the beliefs of Jesus, and also about his very human and clever tactics.

We have to recognise as fundamental what the Church does not want to know about, the political circumstances as these affected Jesus. His country had become incorporated in the Roman empire as part of the Province of Syria. Anyone in that Empire claiming to be a king without authorization by the emperor and the senate was guilty of high treason against Rome and liable to the death penalty. Consequently, if Jesus at the outset of his activities had claimed to be the Messiah he would promptly have been arrested by the Roman authorities and executed. Believing himself to be the Messiah he employed the language of the mystics which would convey nothing in a political sense and spoke of himself habitually as the Son of Man, which simply meant in every day use a human being. Similarly, in speaking publicly on the dangerous theme of the Kingdom of God,

Jesus deliberately spoke in parables because of informers who might be in his audience, saying advisedly: "Let him who can catch my meaning do so."

The parables Jesus explained privately to his disciples, but his own status he did not reveal to them until he was ready to go to Jerusalem to be arrested at the end of his campaign.

In the meantime he applied himself to his task of calling Israel to repentance, so that his people could fulfil their mission of being a light to the Gentiles. He deliberately chose twelve assistants to represent the twelve tribes of Israel. Except for the Jewish pilgrim festivals, Passover, Pentecost and Tabernacles, Jesus never went into Judea himself. He remained in freedom-loving Galilee where he would be much safer. He made his headquarters at Capernaum on the shore of the Sea of Galilee. Several of those he chose were fishermen with boats on the lake, so that an avenue of escape was open to him in case of necessity. Such burly men were also a body-guard, and at least two of his intimates were Zealots, members of the Jewish freedom party.

Only when Jesus had done all he could to influence his people did he carry out his intention to reveal himself publicly as Messiah in Jerusalem. He took his intimates aside, and asked them whom the people believed him to be. The answers were wide of the mark. Then he asked for their view, and Peter burst out, "You are the Messiah." It was an inspired response, as Jesus agreed. He then disclosed to them part of what would be the outcome at Jerusalem. He did not take them entirely into his confidence. But from one Gospel we learn that in the previous winter he had been in Jerusalem at the festival of Chanukah, and evidently he had made his dispositions with close friends which he kept to himself.

The time came for the final journey of Jesus to Jerusalem with the pilgrim bands from the north to keep the Passover there, the Jewish festival of freedom. There was a revealing incident on the way. At Jericho a blind beggar cried out, "Jesus, Son of David, take pity on me." The people tried to silence him. Such language was dangerous. But he would not be silent. On previous occasions when sick people had addressed him as king, Jesus had shut them up. This time he did not do so. A tense atmosphere was created, and not long after Jesus put into operation what he had planned with the help of close friends at Bethany. An ass had been left tethered at the entrance of the village, and Jesus sent two of his disciples with orders to fetch it. They followed his instructions and brought the ass, and he mounted it. The significance of this was immediately perceived. There was a prophecy relating to the advent of Israel's king, riding on an ass (*Zech.* ix. 9). The cry went down the pilgrim line, "Hosanna! Blessed is he that cometh in the name of the Lord."

There was no disguising now that Jesus claimed to be king of Israel. This was an open defiance of Rome.

Even so the authorities were not immediately aware of what was going forward. At this season there were many Jewish pilgrim contingents coming to Jerusalem for the festivals chanting hymns and slogans. Some Pharisees did shout a warning to Jesus, but it went unheeded. Even if the authorities acting for Rome had been alerted they would have needed to exercise caution. At the Passover season there was always the grave danger of a popular uprising against the Occupying Power, and Jerusalem was so packed with pilgrims that this would have involved not only wholesale slaughter but risk to the fabric of the Temple itself, which was overlooked by Roman guards on the adjoining Tower of Antonia. Jesus was perfectly ready, and in fact did, with the advantage of the presence of thousands of his people, cleanse the Temple's outer court of the moneychangers and sellers of sacrificial animals, a business run at a handsome profit by agents of the Sadducean chief priests. The people applauded him, and their slogans against the chief priests have been preserved:

Down with the Boethusians!
Down with their bludgeons!
Down with the Hanaites!
Down with the viper hissings!
Down with the Kantherites!
Down with their libels!
Down with the family of Ishmael ben Pheabi!
Down with their blows with the fist!
They themselves are high priests;
Their sons are treasurers;
Their sons-in-law are captains of the Temple,
And their servants strike the people with staves.

(*Talmud, Pesach* [Passover] fol. 57a)

The writer has need to stress the real position here, since the Church has represented that, as regards the trial of Jesus before Pontius Pilate, the Roman governor, the Jewish people and the chief priests were on the same side. This is totally untrue.

We have to note how intelligently Jesus acted, so that there was no question of his immediate arrest. During the day he was surrounded by multitudes of patriotic Jewish pilgrims. There were so many that multitudes were forced to camp outside Jerusalem. Its environs were covered with tents. They intervened between Jesus at Bethany and the authorities, and he was most careful never to spend a night in the city, when conceivably he might have been secretly arrested or assassinated. Each day before the city gates were closed for the night he had gone to stay with his friends at Bethany. What his plans were he had concealed even from his closest associates, since it was required of him that he should keep the Passover in Jerusalem.

Two essentials were needed. The first was a house in Jerusalem where he would be able with his disciples to celebrate the Passover in the traditional manner. The second was that the owner of such a house should be so devoted to him that Jesus could trust him with his life. Both needs had been provided for in advance on the visit of Jesus to Jerusalem the previous winter, and even the closest of his followers had not been told about them. One of them, Judas, had already formed an intention to betray him, so the precaution was clearly essential.

What took place was like a cloak and dagger story. When the disciples asked where they should prepare the Passover, Jesus sent two of them into Jerusalem, and told them they would be met by a man carrying a water pot. Normally this was done by women. They were to follow that man, and he would lead them to a certain house. There they were to recite to the householder the question, "Where is the guestchamber where I shall eat the Passover with my disciples?" They would then be shown an upstairs room, where they were to prepare.

We could continue much further the account of how Jesus laid his plans to achieve his objectives, and the writer has done so in his books *The Passover Plot* and *After the Cross*. Jesus was fully aware that, once he had publicly owned himself to be king of the Jews, and allowed himself to be arrested in circumstances which he himself had determined, the Roman governor, a cruel man and well-known Jew-hater, would condemn him to be crucified. His crime was not claiming to be divine, but claiming to be king of the Jews, high treason against Rome. The charge against him was duly nailed to his cross.

But Jesus believed from the Scriptures that the Messiah would not be left in a grave and suffer corruption (*Ps.* xvi.10). He must there-fore make his dispositions to assure this. Here another friend in Jerusalem, the Jewish senator Joseph of Arimathea, was called upon secretly to play his part. If events had simply been left to take their course Jesus, with the two who were crucified with him, would have had his limbs broken and his body would have been thrown into a common grave and covered with soil. Survival would have been out of the question. The breaking of limbs was a Roman custom to expedite death, which otherwise would have taken place possibly after two days. Physical recovery then, though exceptionally it had been known, would have been virtually impossible. It was consequently of the utmost importance for Jesus that he should not suffer on the cross for more than a very few hours. In Israel, apparently, crucified Jews were not left on the cross over the Sabbath, by arrangement with the Romans. Jesus had seen to it that even with the greatest expe-dition, he would not be long on the cross before the onset of the Sabbath.

There were therefore two requirements of the situation for which Jesus had in faith to provide. The first was that before the soldiers should be ordered to break the legs of the victims he should seem to have already died, and therefore this would not happen to him. The second was that his body should come into friendly hands, so that he would not be choked to death in the ground, covered with soil.

It would appear from the available information that the first need was met by having someone of the onlookers administer a potion to Jesus, when he called out, "I am thirsty." The second, it was hoped to meet by Joseph of Arimathea going to Pilate and begging for the body of Jesus. Quite naturally Pilate was surprised that Jesus should be dead so soon. But the status of his supplicant allowed him to grant the request. We notice another of the essential requirements for Jesus's escape from death. The tomb in which he was laid was close to the place of crucifixion, and it was above ground, not beneath, so that it received fresh air. It belonged to Joseph, and would probably have been fitted with ledges. The entrance was covered by a circular stone, which ran in a groove, and could only be opened from outside. The body of Jesus had been anointed with spices, which would keep his wounds clean and help them to heal.

The plan would clearly be for Joseph and his associates to open the tomb on Saturday night and remove Jesus to a safe place where his wounds would be treated. We shall be going further into what transpired in the next chapter. There was no element of fraud in the plan, but there was one of faith, in the promise "Thou wilt shew me the path of life" (*Ps.* xvi.11). We have to get used to the idea that Jesus believed that he must fulfil the Messianic programme deriving from interpretation of the Scriptures, and employed his brains to this end. We may regard this as an obsession on his part; but it does tell us a great deal about him as a person.

We have to approach Jesus and his activities from his Messianic Jewish viewpoint, not from a Christian theological one.

It was a tremendously responsible and difficult undertaking to which Jesus was committed, and we must not underestimate what it called for in planning and observation. Even his own family, his widowed mother and brothers, thought he must be deranged. But he was being completely logical from the viewpoint of Messianic conviction.

From the synoptic Gospels we can gain an impression of the political and social circumstances he was up against, and the obstacles he had to overcome. As we have understood, his Messianic mission was "to the lost sheep of the house of Israel". The Prodigal Son had to be brought back and reconciled to his Father. This was because it was Redeemed Israel's task to redeem the nations. Others knew this as well as Jesus, and it was a passport to isolation and hypocrisy.

The Essenes chose to abandon society in general in order to create the Good Society in isolation in wilderness communities, thus leaving the lost sheep of Israel to their fate. Jesus would have none of this mysteriousness and secretiveness. "What I tell you in darkness, speak ye in light; and what ye hear in the ear, that shout from the housetops." The whole of the charge given by Jesus to his disciples (*Matt.* x) is eloquent of his knowledge of what they would be up against in the present state of Jewish affairs.

The Pharisees did not abandon the people to their fate, but in being ultra-orthodox, displaying in an ostentatious manner their piety and holiness, some would live a lie. Being *frum* would conceal sinful private behaviour.

Jesus gave all his love to his suffering people and his mission to them. And though there were women in his company, and he was fond of children, he never married. Everything was concentrated on the programme he must follow as Messiah, and in a short space of time. He was no recluse, and enjoyed the good things of life, visiting people and attending banquets. Yet he was inevitably intensely lonely.

He was surrounded by those to whom, as we have seen, he was unable to confide that he was the Messiah, and often sought solitude and prayer to escape the pressures of crowds and individuals seeking benefits from him. As soon as he could disclose that he was Israel's king there was a move by close associates to request seats on his right hand and left hand in his kingdom. The associates which circumstances required him to choose were ill-educated working-class people, who in deeper matters would more readily get things wrong as right. And in the end, when it came to the crunch, they would abandon him.

It speaks enormously for Jesus's strength of character and his spiritual confidence, that he could face all the problems confronting him religiously, socially and politically, at a most critical time for his country and people. We can only take off our hats to such a man, a king indeed, a man who discovered the meaning of the Messianic for mankind, and conscientiously put it into operation as he understood it.

# 12
# Myth and Legend

By a strange chance, when the writer was working on the previous chapter, there appeared in the British press reference to a report just put out by the House of Bishops of the Anglican Church. This dealt with beliefs, notably the Virgin Birth of Jesus and his Resurrection. On these matters the real issues were dodged. Either those concerned were bad scholars, or their findings were tainted with hypocrisy. We have already noted how things were changed after the Jewish War with the Romans which ended in AD 70. The Jewish government of the Church virtually ceased, and was replaced by non-Jewish Christians with a pagan background. The consequence was that Jesus as Jewish Messiah, a man with a singular function but no more than man, went into the background, to be replaced by a Jesus who was God incarnate. Once this had happened, and since for all Christians Jesus was unique, everything about him would have to be treated as singular, not comparable with what related to anyone else. His 'incarnate deity' could not be compromised in any way, or by any subterfuge. Hence the dilemma of the modern Christian. It is all or nothing.

The only hope of remedy now would have to be (a) the restoration of the Messianic in its Jewish character, and this the Church is not yet ready to face, and (b) the recognition that both in Jewish and Gentile literature of the time of Jesus it had become customary to adorn the births and deaths of the famous, and even their careers, with myth and legend. The fictitious nature of such embellishment was understood by intellectuals, though the uneducated might be ready to take the information which reached them literally. There is material in abundance to make the truth clear from Classical literature and inscriptions. Why should the bishops not say so, and instruct the man and woman in the pew?

We propose to offer here a selection of quotations from ancient sources, first Jewish and then Pagan, under each of two headings: Nativity Legends and Translation Legends.

## Nativity Legends

Our first quotation is from a fragment of manuscript relating to the birth of Noah found among the Dead Sea Scrolls (tr. Yigael Yadin). Bat-Enosh, wife of Lamech, is pregnant:

> I [Lamech] thought in my heart that the conception had been from the Watchers [angelic persons]... and my heart was changed because of this child. Then I, Lamech was frightened and I came to Bat-Enosh, my wife, and [I said], '[Swear to me] by the Most High... Tell me without lies...' When Bat-Enosh, my wife, perceived that my countenance had changed... Then she suppressed her wrath and spoke to me and said, 'O my lord and O my [brother]... I swear to thee by the great Holy One, the King of Heaven... that thine is this seed and from thee is this conception and from thee was the fruit formed... And it is no stranger's, nor is it of any of the Watchers or of the Sons of Heaven...'

Of the birth of Abraham, Jewish legend tells:

> On the night he was born, Terah's [i.e. his father's] friends were feasting in his house, and on leaving late at night they observed a star which swallowed up four other stars from the four sides of the heaven. They forthwith hastened to [King] Nimrod and said: 'Of a certainty a lad has been born who is destined to conquer this world and the next; now, then, give to his parents as large a sum of money as they wish for the child, and then kill him.' [Terah admits he has had a son] but went home and hid him in a cave for three years. (*Jewish Encyclopaedia*, article *Abraham*)

> God begets nothing for himself... I will give as a warrant for my words one that none can dispute, Moses the holiest of men. For he shows us Sarah conceiving at the time when God visited her in her solitude (*Gen.* xxi.1), but when she brings forth it is not to the author of her visitation, but to him who seeks to win wisdom, whose name is Abraham. (Philo, *On the Cherubim*, xiii)

> Tamar too (*Gen.* xxxviii); she bore within her womb the divine seed, but had not seen the sower. For we are told that at that

hour she veiled her face, just as Moses when he turned aside fearing to look upon God (*Exod.* iii). But she closely scanned the symbols and tokens, and judging in her heart that these were the gifts of no mortal she cried aloud, 'To whomsoever these belong, he it is by whom I am with child.' (Philo, *On the Change of Names,* xxiii)

There were a number of Jewish legends of the birth of Moses, from which we may quote:

And Pharaoh told that... he had seen in his dream, and, behold, all the land of Egypt was placed in one scale of a balance, and a lamb... was in the other scale; and the scale with the lamb in it overweighed. Forthwith he sent and called all the magicians of Egypt, and imparted to them his dream. Immediately, Jannes and Jambres, the chief of the magicians, opened their mouths and answered Pharaoh, 'A certain child is about to be born in the congregation of Israel, by whose hand will be the destruction of all the land of Egypt.' Therefore did Pharaoh... give counsel to the Jewish midwives... and said, 'When you attend Jewish women, and see them bear, if it be a male child, you shall kill him.' (*Targum of Palestine*)

God appeared to Amram in a dream, and said, 'I will provide for you all what is for your good, and particularly for thyself what shall make thee famous, for that child, out of dread of whose nativity the Egyptians have doomed the Israelite children to destruction, shall be this child of thine, and he shall be concealed from those who watch to destroy him: and when he is brought up in a surprising way, he shall deliver the Hebrew nation... His memory shall be famous while the world lasts.' When the vision had informed him of these things, Amram awakened and told it to Jochebed his wife. (Josephus, *Antiq.* II. 215-216)

According to the *Chronicles of Jerahmeel*, when Moses was born the whole house was filled with a great light. There were folk tales in the time of Jesus of the births of other Jewish heroes. In the case of Samson we have again a suspicion of the father that his wife had committed adultery (cf. *Matt.* i. 19-20)

When we turn to Pagan legends we learn how Perseus was born of a virgin (Justin Martyr, *Dialogue with Trypho,* 70). Alexander the Great was the product of a union between a god and his mother. A

77

story was told of a serpent which kept company with Olympias while she slept. Her husband Philip saw this and consulted the Delphic Oracle, which informed him that the god Jupiter Ammon had consorted with his wife in the form of a serpent. We have also the story of the birth of the famous sage Apollonius of Tyana. It was related that the god Proteus appeared to his mother before his birth. She was not afraid, but asked him what sort of child she would bear. 'Myself,' he replied. 'And who are you?' she inquired. 'I am Proteus the god of Egypt,' he told her. (The Alexander legend comes from Plutarch, while Philostratus wrote the *Life of Apollonius*.)

Then we have the famous lines of the Roman poet Virgil:

Now is come the last age of the song of Cumae; the great line of the centuries begins anew. Now the Virgin returns, the reign of Saturn returns; now a new generation descends from heaven on high. Only do thou, pure Lucina, smile on the birth of the child, under whom the iron brood shall first cease, and a golden race spring up throughout the world! Thine own Apollo now is king! (*Eclogue* IV)

## Translation Legends

Until close to the time of Jesus there had not developed among the Jews any belief in a home in Heaven for the righteous. Man's destiny was a transformed Earth which the righteous would inherit, so that the idea of a human being taken up to Heaven in a physical sense, as in the case of the Prophet Elijah, was unique. Subsequently contact with other faiths did lead to a view that translation might take place in exceptional cases, but not permanently. Like Elijah, the honoured individual was expected at the appropriate time to return to Earth, by a reincarnation.

A work extant in the time of Jesus told of the Assumption of Moses. Therefore it could be held by the Jewish followers of Jesus as the Messiah that in a revived body he had been taken to Heaven visibly. His stay on high, however, would again be only temporary, and *Psalm* 110 was quoted, "The Lord said unto my Lord [the king], 'Sit thou at my right hand, until I make thine enemies thy footstool.'" At that time Jesus would return to Earth to reign.

Pagan belief, however, found it natural that the eminent should have an eternal home with the gods. And this was to colour Christian convictions of Jesus as these became Gentilised.

We should be aware especially of what was related of Romulus the eponymous founder of Rome:

Of Romulus, when he vanished, was neither the least part of his body, nor rag of his clothes to be seen; so that some fancied that the Senators having fallen upon him, cut his body into pieces, and each took a part away in his bosom. Others think his disappearance was neither in the temple of Vulcan, nor with the Senators only present; but that it happened as he was haranguing the people without the city, near a place called the Goats' Marsh; and that on the sudden most wonderful disorders and alterations beyond belief arose in the air; for the face of the sun was darkened, and the day was turned into an unquiet and turbulent night, made up of thunderings and boisterous winds, raising tempests from all quarters, which scattered the rabble and made them fly, but the Senators kept close together.

The tempest being over, and the light breaking out, when the people gathered again, they missed and enquired for their king; but the Senators would not let them search, or busy themselves about the matter, but commanded them to honour and worship Romulus, as one taken up to the Gods, and who, after having been a good prince, was not to be to them a propitious deity. The multitude hearing this went away rejoicing and worshipping him, in hopes of good things from him.

But there were some canvassing the matter more severely and rigorously who accused and aspersed the Patricians, as men who persuaded the people to believe ridiculous tales, when they themselves were the murderers of the King. Things being in this disorder, one, they say, of the Patricians, of a noble family, and most approved conversation, and withal a most faithful and familiar friend of Romulus himself, who came with him from Alba, Julius Proculus by name, stepping into the company, and taking an oath by all that was most sacred, protested before them all that Romulus appeared to and met him travelling on the road, comelier and fairer than ever, dressed in shining and flaming armour.

And he, being affrighted at the apparition, said, 'Upon what occasion and resentments, O King, did you leave us here, liable to most unjust and wicked surmises, and the whole city destitute, in most bitter sorrow?' And that he made answer, 'It pleased the Gods, O Proculus, that after we had remained a reasonable time among men, and built a city, the greatest in the world both in empire and glory, we should again return to Heaven from whence we came. But be of good heart, and let the Romans know that by the exercise of temperance and fortitude they shall arrive at the highest pitch of human power, and we will be to you the propitious God Quirinus.

This seemed very credible to the Romans, both upon the honesty and oath of him that spoke it; and a certain divine passion, like an enthusiasm, seized on all men, for nobody contradicted it; but laying aside all jealousies and detractions, they prayed to Quirinus, and saluted him God. (Plutarch, *Parallel Lives*)

This kind of material is of the stuff of the Gospel resurrection stories of around the same period. They are typical of their time in a Gentile atmosphere, and there is no reason for attaching more credence to one than to another.

The Romans had initially been rather sceptical of this kind of Near-Eastern embroidery with which the lives of great men were honoured. But they fell in with it since it held the Empire together.

I may quote other instances, borrowing from a previous book of mine. Seneca the philosopher, in his *Apocolocyntosis*, speaks of assumptions: "You demand evidence?" he says. "Right. Ask the man who saw Drusilla en route for Heaven. He will tell you that he saw Claudius [the lame Roman Emperor] going up too, cloppety-cloppety in his usual fashion. That man just can't help seeing what goes on in the sky."

Of the first-century sage Apollonius of Tyana it was told that he had manifested himself after death, and some held that he had become a god and had not died.

The theologian is out of place in such matters. The historian has to place them in their contemporary setting and period atmosphere. A keen analysis of the tales has to recover what circumstances may underlie them as actual happenings.

As regards Jesus, we have the telling incidental evidence I have given in *The Passover Plot* and *After the Cross*, that he had planned that he would not die on the cross and after care for his wounds in a secret place would rejoin his followers in Galilee. In the event it was the miscarriage of the plan that laid the foundations for the legends of his resurrection and ascension. What had not been anticipated was that a keen Roman soldier would stab the body of Jesus before handing it over to Joseph of Arimathea. This incident is only recorded in the Fourth Gospel, since John the Priest (not the Apostle) had been present and witnessed it. None of the Twelve had been there: they were in hiding from the Romans.

The consequence was that early on the Sunday morning when the tomb was opened by Joseph and his associates to bring Jesus out and attend to his wounds at an Essene centre, it was presently found that he was already dead or beyond recovery. His body, therefore, had to be secretly buried. What was left for the women of Jesus's company to find later on Sunday morning was the mystery of an open and empty tomb. An Essene, robed in white, posted there in accordance with the plan and who did not know Jesus had died in the meantime, tried to give the message that Jesus would see his disciples in Galilee. But the women were afraid and ran away. This is one element in the tale we are required to unravel.

# 13

# *Eve of a New Era*

For the Jewish People the period from around 100 BC to AD 100, by Christian reckoning, was perhaps the most significant in their history. It signified not simply the end of an age, but the end of all the Ages. The seers were most active, interpreting the Signs, physical and political, pouring out books in which the names of the heroes and saints of old were requisitioned both to interpret the Signs and to offer moral instruction in preparation for the New Era. There was much talk of judgment on the wicked and the heathen, and the widespread conviction of a leadership vested in Messianic personalities.

One may speculate whether, if the atmosphere had not been like this, individuals like Jesus, John the Baptist, and others, would have made the response that they did. Readings of the New Testament ought to be, but rarely are, aware of the Last Days fervour, with the pious watching every incident, every circumstance of nature, to ascertain when the climax was to be anticipated.

It made sense that a ruthless pagan power, that of Rome, was dominant at this time, that there were evil princes like the Herodians, and mercenary priests like the Ananites, all of them, as it were, leagued together by Satan.

The canvas of the inquirer has inevitably to be much larger, more filled with detail, than Christians normally utilize. Getting at the facts is not difficult if one is prepared to delve into the available records of the period, and to do so without prejudgement or prejudice. Of course, this means treating the New Testament documents no differently than other ancient sources of information, determining initially their date, provenance and validity. The believer in the Christian religion is necessarily excluded from access to the circumstances since he has commitments to an ill-informed and artificially created interpretation. However, there is hope that he can be tempted by such a study as this to open his mind.

In this respect the first thing to be assimilated is that the New Testament records are varied, often contradictory, and fictitious or ill-informed. All the Gospels were written for pagan converts in other lands than Israel, when the Jewish homeland had been devastated by the Roman armies and the Jewish followers of Jesus were dead or scattered. None of the Gospels nor the *Acts of the Apostles* was written before AD 75, nearly half a century and more after the activities of Jesus; and we have no manuscripts of them until at least two hundred years later still, when Christianity had become a new religion alien to Judaism.

As regards the New Testament we are therefore only partially in touch with what really happened, and what is worse we have to take account not only of invention but of forgery. Already in Paul's time he had to speak of forged letters purporting to be from him, and he was forced to add his salutations in his own handwriting (*II. Thess.* ii.2, and iii.17). Similarly the author of the *Revelation* (xxii.18-19) had to put a curse on anyone who added or subtracted from the text. But warnings did not stop the practice. Towards the end of the second century we have a declaration of Dionysius, bishop of Corinth, stating: "As the brethren desired me to write epistles, I did so, and these the apostles of the devil have filled with tares, exchanging some things and adding others, for whom there is a woe reserved. It is not, therefore, matter of wonder, if some have also attempted to adulterate the sacred writings of the Lord, since they have attempted the same in other works that are not to be compared with these" (quoted by Eusebius, *The History of the Church*, IV. xxiii).

In the translation of Jewish apocryphal literature made by Christians we find many instances of falsification of the text in the interest of Christianity. Here are a few examples from the *Testaments of the XII Patriarchs*. The interpolations are within square brackets.

> Then shall I (i.e. Simeon) arise in joy, and will bless the Most High because of His marvellous works, [because God has taken a body and eaten with men and saved men]. (*Test. Sim.* vi.7)

> I (i.e. Levi) am clear from your ungodliness and transgressions, which ye shall commit in the end of the ages [against the saviour of the world, Christ, acting godlessly] deceiving Israel, and stirring up against it great evils from the Lord. (*Test. Levi* xviii.1-7)

> For our father Israel is pure from the transgressions of the chief priests [who shall lay their hands upon the saviour of the world]. (*Test. Levi* xiv. 2)

> Then shall the Lord raise up a new priest... And the glory of the Most High shall be uttered over him, and the spirit of understanding and sanctification shall rest upon him [in the water]. (Test. Levi xviii. 1-7)

Christians may find it difficult to credit that works they have regarded as inspired contain inventions and falsifications; but the matter is beyond dispute. Where propaganda was concerned, the 'saints' could and did manipulate things to suit their interests.

Christian doctrine has not to be in our minds at all as we seek to enter into the feelings and convictions of large sections of the Jewish people in the time of Jesus and for a century or more later. There was no clear pattern of how events would shape themselves, convictions varied. But there was a brooding sense of climax, of impending doom and heavenly intervention. The power of the anti-God enemy, revealed as the Roman empire, would be broken, and many thousands of Jewish Zealots were very ready to make their contribution by propaganda and militancy.

And let us not imagine that the Christians in Israel stood apart from this: they were in the very thick of it; for was it not Jesus their king who would replace Caesar and doom his legions to destruction? The *Apocalypse of Jesus Christ*, commonly known as the *Revelation*, offers one version of what was still being anticipated at the end of the first century AD. Imagined Christian charity does not enter into the contemplation of the fate of Rome, that great whore Babylon.

> 'Treat her as she has treated you,' cries a voice from heaven, 'and doubly so, in accordance with her deeds. In the very goblet she mixed for others, mix double for her. To the extent that she has glorified herself and waxed wanton, by so much render to her anguish and sorrow. For she says to herself, I sit a queen, and am no widow. Sorrow I shall never know. Therefore in a single day her plagues shall come, death and sorrow, and famine, and by fire she shall be consumed; for mighty is the Lord God who judges her' (*Rev.* xviii).

Yes, reader, this and much more is in the New Testament.

But let us turn to another apocalyptic work, of Jewish authorship but approved by many in the Early Church, the *Apocalypse of Baruch*.

This is very good in reflecting the atmosphere of the first century AD and especially, like the New Testament Apocalypse, that which prevailed after the Jewish War and the Fall of Jerusalem in AD 70 when Rome had triumphed.

Before the advent of the Kingdom of God there would be the Great Tribulation. The seer of the *Apocalypse of Baruch* is told:

> Into twelve parts is that time divided, and each one of them is reserved for what is appointed for it. In the first part there will be the beginning of commotions. And in the second part there will be slayings of the great ones. And in the third part there will be the fall of many by death. And in the fourth part the sending of desolation. And in the fifth part famine and the withholding of rain. And [seventh part missing]. And in the eighth part a multitude of portents and incursions of the Shedim [i.e. demons]. And in the ninth part the fall of fire. And in the tenth part rapine and much oppression. And in the eleventh part wickedness and unchastity. And in the twelfth part confusion from the mingling together of all these things aforesaid. (xxvii.1-13)

The final stages will be when "the last leader of that time [the Antichrist] will be left alive, when the multitudes of his hosts will be put to the sword, and he will be bound, and they will take him up to Mount Zion, and My Messiah will convict him of all his impieties, and will gather and set before him all the works of his hosts. And afterwards he will put him to death, and protect the rest of My people which shall be found in the place which I have chosen. And his principate will stand for ever, until the world of corruption is at an end, and until the times aforesaid are fulfilled." (xl. 1-3)

The circumstances of Pentecost, as may be glimpsed, though only partially, from the *Acts of the Apostles*, recognize the awesome knowledge that the Last Times had now actually started. They would move speedily and inevitably towards their climax. Therefore now was the time for all Israelites to repent of their evil deeds and rally to the banner of the Messiah. The Jewish festival of Pentecost, one of the three pilgrim feasts, celebrated the first fruits of harvest, and thus most appropriately could signify those who now pledged their allegiance to the ultimate king of Israel. We are told of many thousands of Jews, both men and women, who believed, and a great number of the priests.

But we have to get much closer to the circumstances than the *Acts* relates. There is a hint of the beginnings of the organization of the faithful Israelites, centred on Jerusalem. And it is one which one could hardly expect the untutored Galilean associates of Jesus to have devised. They could employ one, however, which was already in being and highly suitable, and which we have only been able to learn about in the present century. This, as we have already noted, was the Essene organization, which also claimed to represent the "faithful remnant" of Israel of the Last Times. I may quote here from Vermes, *The Dead Sea Scrolls in English*:

> The most important of their festivals was the Feast of Weeks [i.e. Pentecost], the Feast of the Renewal of the Covenant. Its ritual is described at the beginning of the *Community Rule* and in an unpublished section of the *Damascus Rule*. Opening the ceremony, the Priests and Levites offer blessing to God, and those entering the Covenant with them reply 'Amen, Amen.' The priests go on to recall the past favours of God, and the Levites follow them with a recital of Israel's transgressions. This culminates in a public confession. 'We have strayed! We have disobeyed!' etc., after which the penitents are blessed by the Priests. Then the Levites pronounce a long curse on the 'lot of Satan', and with the Priests they solemnly adjure all those whose repentance is incomplete not to enter the Covenant. 'Cursed be the man,' they say, 'who enters this Covenant while walking among the idols of his heart... He shall be cut off from the midst of the Sons of Light... and his lot shall be among them that are cursed for ever.' (*Community Rule*, I, II)

The penitents, who gave all their possessions to the Community, were also known, as Paul and the authors of the fundamental Gospel convey, as 'the Poor' (Ebionim). The fate is told in the *Acts* of Ananias and his wife Sapphira, who did "walk among the idols of their hearts, and kept back part of the price".

For the Essenes Pentecost was particularly the festival of the Renewal of the Covenant. Consequently, at this time annually, a general assembly of members was held, when their status was reassessed in the light of their behaviour, reports from different communities were given to the central authority, and so on. The Party of Jesus adopted the system for their own requirements. The Pharisees had a similar one. As we have seen, for the Nazoreans there was a Council at Jerusalem composed of the Apostles and Elders, under the Presidency of James, the brother of Jesus, assisted by two others, initially Peter and John the Priest. To this Council the question of the terms of admission of converted Gentiles was referred, no doubt at the season of Pentecost, when as often as was practicable Paul had to leave his mission field to report his activities to Jerusalem.

Christian teaching has ignored that Paul had to have his status agreed by the Nazorean Jewish Council, and was obliged to report to it at the time of Pentecost if it could be managed (*Acts* xviii.21, xx.16; *I. Cor.* xvi.8).

Good and effective organization was essential if the gigantic task was to be achieved of notifying all Jews in all lands of the Messiah's speedy coming in judgment to establish his kingdom. What we call the Preaching of the Gospel to save souls had this aim in its original objective.

# 14

# *The Great Commission*

Because the Church was effectively to detach the obligation to save souls from Hell from relationship with the Messianic, it has not been understood what really lay behind the burst of evangelism which broke out in the decade from AD 40. To get the correct picture we have to take account of the contemporary circumstances as they affected the Jews, particularly those who were Nazoreans. We have already pointed out how much the pious were under the influence of 'signals' in nature and in political affairs that indicated that the Last Times were now in train prior to the advent on Earth of the Kingdom of God. Multitudes were affected by this excitement.

Unfortunately, the Church was to become so paganized and anti-semitic that it was to become a religion instead of a Messianic enterprise. This position would be so ingrained, indeed, that the Christian reader of today will find it extremely difficult to rectify his habitual way of thinking, especially as it has support in trusted New Testament statements, which in fact were wilful falsifications. However, we must make an effort to set the record straight.

Christian missionary enterprise has been particularly stimulated by sayings attributed to Jesus at the end of the Gospels of *Matthew* and *Mark*. The first runs in the King James version: "Go ye therefore, and teach all nations, baptizing them in the name of the Father, and of the Son, and of the Holy Ghost: teaching them to observe all things whatsoever I have commanded you: and, lo, I am with you alway, even unto the end of the world. Amen." The second, in *Mark*, reads: "And he [Jesus] said unto them, Go ye into all the world, and preach the gospel to every creature. He that believeth and is baptized shall be saved; but he that believeth not shall be damned." Both statements are Christian inventions, the latter is one of alternative Markan endings found in manuscripts.

It is in fact the New Testament itself which proves the falsehood of these invented sayings, as can readily be ascertained. The one from *Matthew* is clearly designed to set aside what Jesus had actually told his disciples during his ministry: "Go not into the way of the Gentiles... Go instead to the lost sheep of the house of Israel. And as ye go, proclaim, 'The Kingdom of Heaven is at hand' " (*Matt.* x. 5-7). The mission of the apostles was exclusively to the Jews, to advise them of the near advent of the Messianic Era.

This is fully confirmed by the *Acts of the Apostles*. First we find a problem for the followers of Jesus created by the faith of the centurion Cornelius, even though he had actually abandoned paganism. Peter, himself, who had been so intimate with Jesus, had to be given a special vision to enable him to receive Cornelius into the Christian community. He would have had no problem at all, or the other apostles, if they had known the post-resurrection sayings of Jesus we have quoted. Neither would there have been the much more heated controversy over the reception of Gentiles created by the activities of Paul, when the apostles and leaders of the Christian Community refused to recognise converts from the Gentiles as fellow-Israelites, only as 'strangers within the gates', unless they observed the laws of Moses.

Then we have to face up to what exactly is the Gospel, the Good News. According to the Bible it is the information to Israel that in Jesus the awaited Messiah has appeared, and consequently the deliverance of Israel and the advent on Earth of the Kingdom of God, were at hand. This had specific concern for the Jews, who according to Scripture would be the instruments for bringing all nations to God, and thus to an era of peace and justice.

One of the Christian falsifications in the New Testament, in this case in the Authorised (King James) Version, is concerned with this very matter. In the Messianic Birth Story in *Luke* an angel appears to the Jewish shepherds near Bethlehem, and tells them, "I bring you glad tidings of great joy, which shall be to all people. For unto you is born this day in the city of David a Saviour, which is Christ the Lord" (ii. 10-11). Glad tidings is of course the same thing as Gospel, and it is the Good News to Israel that the long-awaited Messiah, the ultimate king of Israel, has appeared. But this was not what the Christian translators wanted to represent. They put 'Saviour' when they should have said 'deliverer', and 'Christ the Lord' instead of 'anointed lord' or 'lord Messiah'. In the Greek there is no definite article before 'lord', but there *is* a definite article before 'people'. The tidings are 'for all the people', the Jewish people. The translators wanted both to support Christian theology and to make the Gospel apply to people in general 'all people'. So they wilfully dropped the definite article.

The countless Christians who look to the Authorised Version as the very Word of God have not been advised that in many places the language has been falsified. The circumstances are actually very much worse because of large-scale forgery, notably of a great part of the *Gospel of John*. Everything we read in the New Testament has to be very thoroughly investigated before we can employ any of it as evidential.

If we are to be realistic we have to apprehend that what created a sense of urgency among the Jewish followers of Jesus, to inform all Jews everywhere that the Messiah had come, was the way things were shaping.

There had been a succession of events which dictated action. Perhaps the most influential of these had been the design of the Emperor Gaius Caligula to have his statue set up in the Temple at Jerusalem as an object of worship. Petronius, the Roman governor of Syria, had held up carrying this out in response to Jewish protests. The Emperor ordered him to fulfil his command or commit suicide. But by a miracle, as it seemed, this letter only reached Petronius at Antioch after another had come advising him that the Emperor had been assassinated. It was at Antioch that the followers of Jesus were first called Christians (i.e. Messianists).

We have evidence that it was under the next Emperor Claudius, not long after AD 41, that the Community at Jerusalem determined to send emissaries throughout the Roman Empire with news of the Messiahship of Jesus directed to all the Jewish Communities. They carried with them as tradition indicates, two documents in Hebrew not extant in their original form, but utilised by the writers of *Matthew* and *Luke*. One was a collection of Old Testament texts deemed to have been fulfilled by Jesus. The second was a collection of sayings of Jesus (see above, p.65).

Of great service to the Messianic activists was a system, then in vogue, which was under Roman protection. As I have written elsewhere, it had long been customary for the Jewish Sanhedrin to send agents to the Jewish communities abroad, to deal with the collection of the Temple tax and convey instructions on various religious matters. The Romans themselves by their lines of communication on land and sea greatly facilitated the travels of such emissaries, a fact which must have been appreciated as Divine justice by the Messianists and Zealots intent on Rome's overthrow. The militants could utilize these routes to foster rebellion and to collect funds for the purchase of weapons.

It cannot have been at all easy for the Jews in the Roman empire, who were comfortably circumstanced and enjoyed Roman protection, to distinguish between non-militant religious teachers and Zealot agents. The other-worldly Apostle Paul, himself a Roman citizen, in his missionary journeys seems to have been totally blind to what was going on, so that one of the primary causes of Jewish opposition to his teaching was completely misunderstood. It did not dawn on him that in preaching the resurrection of Christ (in Greek *anastasis Christou*) this could be interpreted as 'Messianic uprising'.

And what was more, it was the fact that Paul was collecting funds for the "poor saints" of Jerusalem. No wonder that the threatened Jewish community at Thessalonica informed the Roman authorities against him. "These subverters of the Empire have now reached here, and Jason has harboured them. All of them are violators of Caesar's decrees, and declare there is another king, one Jesus" (*Acts* xvii.7). Some years later Paul was indicted to the Roman governor at Caesarea as "a plague-carrier, a fomenter of revolt among all the Jews of the Empire, a ringleader of the Nazorean Party" (*Acts* xxiv.5).

Church historians have totally failed to appreciate that the Christian apostles were very easily identified with the Jewish Resistance Movement and its agents. The Roman government was not ignorant of these activities. Suetonius the historian wrote that the Emperor Claudius at this time "expelled the Jews from Rome, who were continually making disturbances at the instigation of Chrestus" (Suet. *Claudius* xxv). Dio Cassius, however, says that the Jews were too numerous to expel from the capital without risk, but that Claudius closed the synagogues (Dio Cassius, *Roman History* lx.6). The *Acts* mentions the tent-maker Aquila and his wife Priscilla, who had been among those expelled, and whom Paul met at Corinth (*Acts* xviii.2).

Even Egypt was not immune from the propaganda of the Messianists, Nazoreans and Zealots. There is extant a letter from Claudius to the Jews of Alexandria warning them not to entertain Jewish itinerants from Syria (which embraced Judea), if they did not wish to be treated as abettors of "a pest which threatens the whole world".

I quote here my book *The Pentecost Revolution*: "There was another side to the proclamation of Jesus and the Gospel of the Kingdom than Christians have imaged. Some of those engaged were not like modern missionaries bringing word of the love of God to the heathen as revealed in the death of Jesus Christ. They represented the Church militant in a grimmer sense. They were preparing the Way of the Lord with fanatical zeal by sowing broadcast the seeds of disaffection in the strongholds of the foe."

# 15

# *The Lord's Brother*

The Christian Faith, because it is concerned with a religion in which Jesus figures uniquely as the Son of God, has no room for the historical circumstances of Christian beginnings and chooses to ignore them. At worse it even perverts them. Yet the New Testament still shows that Jesus was of Davidic descent, and that he was the eldest of a family comprising five boys and at least two girls. His brother Jacob (James), as we have seen, would in fact become head of all followers of Jesus and president of its Council at Jerusalem, a person of prominence and historical interest outside Christian circles.

In our pursuit of the Messianic we have to get things in correct perspective, and this necessarily calls for the restoration of the consequential part played by Jacob the Just. He was a saintly Jew who fitted admirably into the Last Times atmosphere of his period, and if we choose to pursue it – as we must – his contribution enables us much more clearly to comprehend the non-militant aspect of Messianism, favoured also by many of the Pharisees and Essenes.

The New Testament collection contains one letter attributed to Jacob. This, however, is not directed to any Christian community but to "the Twelve Tribes of the Dispersion" (the scattered sheep of Israel). Jacob here acts, or is made to act, like the president of the Sanhedrin in his official capacity. There is also extant a forged letter in the name of Clement, first bishop of Rome, written to James as "bishop of bishops, who rules Jerusalem, the holy community of the Hebrews, and the communities everywhere excellently founded by the providence of God."

It must be very evident to any unprejudiced investigator that the immediate family of Jesus played no minor part in the period of Christian beginnings, and that Jacob especially exercised supreme authority in the early days, an authority which one source (*The Gospel of Thomas*) claims had been bestowed upon him by Jesus. Before he left this world the disciples had asked him to whom they should now go, and Jesus had replied, "In the place to which you will go [i.e. Jerusalem], you will go to Jacob the Just, for whose sake heaven and earth were created."

We have to recognize, therefore, that Jerusalem was the first place of authority of the Messianic organization centred on Jesus, and that his brother Jacob was accepted as the head of that authority, assisted by Peter and John (probably John the Priest). The fact that at this time the Jewish followers of Jesus, as the *Acts* proclaim, were strict observers of the Laws of Moses, conveys that they had in Jacob an outstanding example. All the records we have confirm this, so that even Eusebius in his *History of the Church* (4th century) could not set it aside:

> Now Jacob, the brother of the Lord, who, as there were many of this name, was termed the Just by all, from the days of our Lord until now, received the government of the Community with the Apostles. This Apostle was consecrated from his mother's womb. He drank neither wine nor fermented liquors, and abstained from animal food. A razor never came upon his head; he never anointed himself with oil or used a public bath. He alone was allowed to enter the Holy Place. He never wore woollen, only linen garments. He was in the habit of entering the Temple alone, and was often to be found upon his knees and interceding for the forgiveness of the people; so that his knees became as hard as a camel's... And indeed, on account of his exceeding great piety, he was called the Just [i.e. Zadik] and Oblias [i.e. *Ophla-am*), which signifies Justice and the People's Bulwark; as the Prophets declare concerning him. (II. xxiii)

Significantly, the Jewish historian Josephus made reference to the fate of Jacob, though he had provided no details about the death of Jesus. Josephus, whom we shall quote in due course, was a younger contemporary of Jacob.

But first we have to clarify that the Early Church, especially in its homeland, was much more concerned with politics than with theology. The Messiah was seen democratically as his people's leader, not as a divine autocrat. That is why the Pharisees, who politically were social democrats, were strongly Messianic in their convictions. To the contrary, the chief priests, autocratic and aristocratic, favoured Sadduceeism, which either set aside the idea of a Messiah, or treated the advent of a Davidic Messiah as of secondary importance, subordinate to the High Priest.

Because Christianity was to become hierarchic, Christians have got things all wrong in imagining the Jews of this period to have been subservient to the chief priests, notably in calling upon the Roman governor to crucify Jesus. If the Jewish populace had been present at Pilate's residence, which they could not possibly have been, the last thing they would have wished to heed was the advice of the detested chief priests.

Historically, we have to recognise that the opposition of the Pharisees to the Sadducees was not purely doctrinal. It reflected the kind of distinction we make between Socialism and Conservatism. The followers of Jesus favoured the former. The conflict is echoed in the Church to this day in the guise of Romanism and Protestantism.

But much more than this we have to look at these alignments in the first century AD context of the Roman occupation of Palestine. Neither the Pharisees nor the Sadducees wanted the Roman rule. But the aristocratic Sadducees appreciated that it was convenient to have the Roman authority and troops available to protect them against the militancy of the Jewish populace. The Pharisees themselves were for the most part non-militant: they were believers in Divine intervention to save Israel and overthrow the evil-doers. But very close to them were the Zealots, who were not prepared to wait for action from Heaven and represented a militant Messianism. The ranks of the followers of Jesus included both Pharisees and Zealots, and also many of the poor priests who were exploited by the high priestly families.

For the Pharisees and the Jewish masses Jacob son of Joseph was a symbolic figure. His Jewish piety and Nazorite way of life, joined with the fact of his descent from King David, made him a very positive witness that the promises of God to His people would have their fulfilment, even to those Pharisees who had not accepted the Messiahship of Jesus. In some ways he made a stronger appeal to the Jewish people than his brother had done.

But one of the things which Jesus had done in his Messianic capacity was to challenge the venality of the Temple marketing system with its profitable sale of sacrificial victims and its exchange of idolatrous foreign currency. This earned him popular applause and support, and brought down on him the wrath of the high priesthood, and made them determined on his death as a dangerous rabble-rouser, particularly menacing because of his Messianic pretensions.

Unfortunately for the House of Annas and the chief priests in general the Man had been replaced by a whole Messianic Movement headed by the Man's brother. The appeal of this brother to the nation, both as Saint and the People's Champion, intensified its menace to the hierarchy. From their point of view, unless it could be overcome, war with Rome was inevitable and the Temple with its services would be abolished.

Opportunity was sought to do away with the revered leader of the Nazoreans before it should be too late. This was found in 62 AD when the hierarchy under the high priest Ananus was briefly at the head of Jewish affairs. The Roman governor Festus had died, and his successor had not yet arrived. The circumstances are reported by Josephus in his *Antiquities*:

> Possessed of such a character [i.e. for rashness and daring], Ananus thought he had a favourable opportunity because Festus was dead and Albinus was still on the way. And so he convened the judges of the Sanhedrin and brought before them a man named Jacob, the brother of Jesus who was called the Christ, and certain others. He accused them of having transgressed the Law and delivered them up to be stoned. Those of the inhabitants of the city [Jerusalem] who were considered the most fair-minded and who were strict in the observance of the Law were offended at this. They therefore secretly sent to King Agrippa urging him, for Ananus had not even been correct in his first step, to order him to desist from any further such actions. Certain of them even went to meet Albinus, who was on his way from Alexandria, and informed him that Ananus had no authority to convene the Sanhedrin without his consent. Convinced by these words, Albinus angrily wrote to Ananus threatening to take vengeance upon him. King Agrippa, because of Ananus's action, deposed him from the high priesthood, which he had held for three months, and replaced him with Jesus son of Damnaeus. (*Antiq*. XX. 200-3)

There was another reference to the circumstances elsewhere in the works of Josephus, not in any extant MS, but quoted by Origen and Eusebius. It read: "These things happened to the Jews to avenge Jacob the Just, who was the brother of Jesus called Christ, and whom the Jews had slain, although he was a man most distinguished for his justice." This could have been an early Christian forgery.

We can follow the animus between the chief priests and the Nazoreans ever since Annas the Elder had delivered Jesus to Pontius Pilate. An echo of it reached us in Matthew's Gospel where the opponents of Jesus declare: "His blood be on us, and on our children." But they were never spoken by "all the people" (as in *Matt.* xxvii.25). This falsehood would bring on the Jews untold suffering and hatred through the centuries, and was not sufficiently repudiated in the present century by the Second Vatican Council.

The chief priests certainly did come to a miserable end. Ananus son of Annas with another high priest Jesus son of Gamalas was killed by the Idumeans in the Jewish Revolt. Ananias son of Nedebaeus with his brother Hezekiah was murdered by Menahem the Zealot, a descendant of the patriot Judas of Galilee. Before the Jewish War with the Romans, however, the family to which Jesus belonged escaped from Jerusalem to Syria under the leadership of a first cousin of Jesus, Simeon son of Cleophas. Many of the Nazoreans fled with them.

Curiously, in one of the Dead Sea Scrolls, the *Commentary on Habakkuk*, there is a passage pertinent to all these circumstances. Here the Wicked Priest is delivered into the hands of his enemies because of the iniquity committed against the Teacher of Righteousness and the men of his Council. The money and wealth of the Last Priests of Jerusalem will be delivered into the hands of the army of the Kittim (i.e. the Romans).

There is one more reference to the death of Jacob the brother of Jesus. This occurs in the *History of the Church* (II. xxiii) of Eusebius, quoted from the *Memoirs* of a second-century writer Hegesippus. Part of this passage reads as follows:

> And they began to stone Jacob, as he did not die immediately when cast down; but turning round he knelt down, saying, 'I beseech Thee, O Lord God and Father, forgive them for they know not what they do.' Thus they were stoning him, when one of the priests of the sons of Rechab, a son of the Rechabites spoken of by Jeremiah the prophet, cried out, saying, 'Stop! What are you doing? The Just One is praying for you.'
>
> But one of them, a fuller, beat out the brains of the Just with the club he used to beat out clothes. Thus he suffered martyrdom, and they buried him on the spot where his tombstone still remains, close to the Temple. He became a faithful witness, both to the Jews and Greeks, that Jesus is the Christ. Immediately after this, Vespasian invaded and took Judea.

The prayer attributed to Jacob is credited to Jesus by Luke, but not given in any other Gospel; and it is possible that he took it from the story of the martyrdom of the brother of Jesus.

But, indeed, there is so much in early Christian tradition which is ignored by those of our time who teach about Christian Beginnings. Either they are ignorant, and should not therefore be claiming to give authoritative instruction, or they wilfully refuse to refer to what does not suit their doctrine, and are deliberately misleading, which is very much worse.

# 16

# *The Great Tribulation*

In the sixth decade of the first century AD events in Israel were building up to a climax, largely due to the aggressive and domineering character of the Roman governors, and also their cupidity.

Josephus states: "The administration of Albinus, who followed Festus, was of another order; there was no form of villainy which he omitted to practise... But his successor, Gessius Florus, made him appear by comparison a paragon of virtue... Gessius ostentatiously paraded his outrages upon the nation, and, as though he had been sent as hangman of condemned criminals, abstained from no form of robbery or violence... and almost went the length of proclaiming throughout the country that all were at liberty to practise brigandage, on condition that he received his share of the spoils..." He contemplated the prospect of war with the nation "his only hope of covering up his own enormities. For, if the peace were kept, he expected to have the Jews accusing him before Caesar; whereas, could he bring about their revolt, he hoped that the larger crime would divert inquiry into less serious offences. In order, therefore, to produce an outbreak of the nation, he daily added to their sufferings." (*The Jewish War*, II.277-283)

But there was the other side of the picture. The Jewish revolt from Roman rule was not only due to the behaviour of the Occupying Power. Subservience to heathen domination was spiritually as well as politically intolerable. There was a strong sense of an apocalyptic climax, of both impending judgment and Messianic deliverance. This crisis must surely be the climax of ages. The atmosphere is conveyed in *Matthew* xxiv.

To quote Josephus again: "There arose another body of villains, with purer hands but more impious intentions, who no less than the

99

assassins ruined the peace of the city. Deceivers and impostors, under the pretence of divine inspiration fostering revolutionary changes, they persuaded the multitude to act like madmen, and led them out into the desert under the belief that God would give them tokens of deliverance... The impostors and brigands, banding together, incited numbers to revolt, exhorting them to assert their independence, and threatening to kill any who submitted to Roman domination and forcibly to suppress those who voluntarily accepted servitude" (*Jewish War*, II.253-265).

Already under the Emperor Nero the followers of Jesus as Messiah had been doomed to death by the flames, accused of setting Rome on fire. The manner of death was what the Romans prescribed for the practice of magic and sorcery (Paulus, *Sent.* v). And they could claim justification since the Christians had been predicting the fiery end of Rome, by interpolating the *Sibylline Oracles*. One of the predictions reads: "On thee some day shall come, O haughty Rome, a fitting stroke from heaven, and thou the first shall bend the neck, be levelled to the earth, and fire shall utterly consume thee, bent upon thy pavements. Thy wealth shall perish, and on thy site shall wolves and foxes dwell, and then shalt thou become all desolate as though thou hadst not been... Near at hand is the End of the World, and the Last Day, and judgment of immortal God on behalf of those who are both called and chosen. First of all inexorable wrath shall fall on Rome..." (*Sibylline Oracles*, Bk.VIII; see also above p.59).

Jews and Christians alike, in those days, were ready to believe that the climax of the Ages was imminent. In the War with the Romans that developed in 66 AD the great majority of the places associated with Jesus and his Jewish followers were destroyed, and their inhabitants killed or taken captive. There had been a battle on the Sea of Galilee. At the end the sacred Temple at Jerusalem had perished and its holy vessels carried off to grace a Roman triumph.

This must surely signalise the immanence of the Kingdom of God. And indeed in the first century AD the belief was general that the Kingdom of God was at hand, and consequently the judgments on sinners and great calamities were to be anticipated. Surely the Messiah should now appear, or for Christians reappear!

But incredibly nothing of what was imagined in this respect took place. The judgments had come, but where was the Messiah and the Kingdom of God? The contemporary prophets had got things all wrong, something that has been known to happen in our own times.

The followers of Jesus, especially, were greatly troubled. Their writings sought to excuse the failure of their expectations. The *Second Epistle of Peter* shows full awareness of the situation. In the Last Days scoffers would come, saying, "What has happened to the promise of Christ's coming? Since the fathers fell asleep all things continue as they were from the beginning of the Creation." They were answered by the plea that "One day is with the Lord as a thousand years, and a thousand years as one day. The Lord is not slack concerning his promise, as some men count slackness; but is long suffering to us-ward, not willing that any should perish, but that all should come to repentance." This fake *Second Letter of Peter* in fact answers the *First* where Peter declares (iv.7), "The end of all things is at hand."

The *Acts of the Apostles*, written towards the close of the first century AD also seeks to account for the failure of the Second Advent. Before Jesus is taken to Heaven his followers ask him, "Lord, wilt thou at this time restore again the kingdom to Israel?" They are answered, "It is not for you to know the times or the seasons, which the Father hath put in his own power" (i. 6-7). From the date of the authorship of the *Acts* it would in fact be more than eighteen and a half centuries before Israel repossessed its land.

But what had taken place was a radical and drastic transformation in Jewish and Christian affairs the consequences of which have endured to the present day.

With the Jews, they had not only been deprived of their land and distinct nationality, persisting in what came to be called the Diaspora, they were no longer under a priestly government as this affected their religion. They now came under the spiritual authority of the former Pharisees. The Law of Moses was interpreted and expanded to meet the new Jewish circumstances, giving rise to the Rabbinical Codes of the *Mishnah* and *Gemara*, brought together in the *Talmud*. The synagogues everywhere represented the new Judaism.

This did enable the Jews to persist, even under conditions of severe persecution, mainly from the Christians. And they could cherish the hope of return to the Holy Land and the coming of the Messiah as a vision of the future, more ideal than real. The emphasis was on faith in the One God and Father, whose ways were inscrutable but insured Israel's survival.

These developments of the future were to be expedited by another serious attempt to retrieve Jewish fortunes in the second century AD. This was the insurrection of Bar Cochba, a militant Messiah, in the

101

THE MYSTERY OF THE MESSIAH

reign of the Roman Emperor Hadrian. This struggle was desperate, bitter and prolonged, and the Roman forces triumphed only with the greatest difficulty. The outcome was to complete the political disintegration of the Jews. Jerusalem itself was abolished, and in its place the Romans created a new but smaller city named Ælia Capitolina on a quite different ground plan. From this city Jews were completely excluded, the Jewish followers of Jesus among them. Eventually a small non-Jewish church was allowed to be established.

Persecution of the Christians in the Roman world was virtually to end in the fourth century with the tactical adoption of what had become the Christian Faith by the Emperor Constantine. But by this time Christianity had departed far more from its original positions than had the Jews. It had in fact become a new religion, which persecuted the people from which it had sprung. This religion was a compound of Judaism and Paganism, and largely eliminated the Messianic which supposedly it represented. Such alienism was to give rise to the long drawn out Times of the Gentiles, and not until the twentieth century of the Christian Era would there be a real beginning of setting things to rights.

We shall need to go into some detail to clarify that Christian Orthodoxy was the Great Apostasy, since Ecclesiastical History has not been represented as anti-Christian, except to an extent by Protestants. But they too are nearly as much in error.

# 17
# Christendom Astray

We have had good reason to see that the story of Christian Beginnings down to the fourth century AD owes a very great deal to perversion and misinterpretation. Now we must develop this theme since it is of paramount consequence for the comprehension of the Messianic.

We must revert first of all to what has been disclosed of what the Messianic is all about. Its ultimate aim is to unite the nations of the world in peace and righteousness under the One God and Father of all mankind. To this end there was needed an exemplary people, "a kingdom of priests and a holy nation", both to illustrate what was to be achieved universally and to promote its fulfilment. Except in an earthly context the Messianic never, other than in Christian imagination, had anything to do with saving souls from hell so that they might dwell in heaven. The Messianic was not in itself a religion: it was a programme for our planet.

The people of Israel were chosen by God as the instrument of the Messianic process. To this end the progenitor Abraham was called from Ur of the Chaldees to travel to what would become known as the Holy Land. To learn obedience and respect for the underdog his descendants were to be enslaved in Egypt, one of the great autocratic powers of the time. It was while they were in such circumstances that Moses was sent to tell Pharaoh to free Israel which is God's Firstborn Son. (*Exod.* iv. 22)

In journeying through the wilderness to the Promised Land Israel was given the code which would govern its conduct as a Priestly People, and single them out for the universal function they were designed to perform. This function was illustrated within the camp of Israel by the choice of Levi as a priestly tribe among the other tribes (see Chapter 2).

It was Israel's attempt to escape its responsibilities, and to be just the same as all the other nations, that introduced an individual Messiah in the person of an *anointed* king, Messiah (Christ in Greek) meaning 'anointed one'. The people wanted him as their military leader; but in God's plan the king of Israel would be faithful to the Divine Laws and be the means of bringing his people back to their own Messianic function. No such ideal king would arise in many centuries, though initially David had seemed to come close to reflecting him.

And so there arose, as visioned by the Hebrew prophets, the expectation that one day there would be a Son of David, who like his people would be named God's son and firstborn, and who would be instrumental in bringing them, or at least a loyal remnant, back to their task of being a light to the Gentiles. In the end "the vision would speak and not lie".

Any declared Christian who does not know that these matters are what the Messianic is all about has not properly read his Bible (both Old and New Testaments).

It is unfortunate that as yet we do not have more than a few quotations from any Hebrew Gospel which could have emanated from the land in which Jesus lived. But even with the New Testament we are not altogether deprived of access to the Messianic as Jesus and his followers understood it. Indeed, though its documents for the most part are relatively late and somewhat legendary, and some begin to reflect Gentile influences, it is surprising how much of the true circumstances has got through. The clear evidences had to be acknowledged and respected, even though elements were introduced to counteract them.

The first thing which becomes clear to the honest inquirer is that the New Testament is not about any religion called Christianity originated by Jesus. It is about the fulfilment of the Jewish Messianic Hope in the person of Jesus as king of Israel descended from King David, and it is in this respect that he is described as Christ (the anointed).

That the early Christians were by religion faithful Jews is certified by the *Acts of the Apostles*. Here, for instance, we have Saul, afterwards Paul, preaching in the synagogue at Antioch in Pisidia. He announces that of David's seed "hath God according to his promise raised unto *Israel* a deliverer, Jesus" (*Acts* xiii.23). As we have seen, the Jesus Party in Israel had its government at Jerusalem, consisting

104

of his Apostles and other Jewish elders, headed by Jesus's own brother Jacob (James). It is to this government that Paul had to report on his activities, and particularly about his preaching to Gentiles.

The official 'Christian' response here is very interesting (see Chapter 10). Those who had been closest to Jesus say to Paul, "Thou seest, brother how many thousands [Gr. myriads] of Jews there are which believe [i.e. in the Messiahship of Jesus]; and they all are zealous of the Law [of Moses]: and they are informed of thee, that thou teachest all the Jews that are among the Gentiles to forsake Moses, saying that they ought not to circumcise their children, neither to walk after the customs." (*Acts* xxi. 20-21) The allegation, of course, was false, and to prove it Paul was recommended to purify himself in the Temple with some Christians who were under a vow. This would demonstrate, they told Paul, that "thou also walkest orderly, and keepest the Law." Paul, evidently, had not the slightest hesitation in accepting this suggestion which would prove that he was a loyal and conforming Jew.

There is no sign here of any Christian religion, and those involved had been the immediate associates of Jesus.

The problem raised was that affecting Gentiles who acknowledged Jesus as Messiah. How were they to be regarded? Paul wanted them to be recognised as members of the House of Israel. This would have been perfectly permissible if they were ready to become full proselytes to Judaism, 'Proselytes of Righteousness'. But it did not satisfy Paul. He claimed that as the Messiah had perfectly kept the Law faith in Jesus was sufficient to give believing Gentiles Israelite status. The leaders of Messianic Israel said no. The Law of Moses was binding on all Israelites. What the New Covenant had done was to engrave the Law on the hearts of all God's People so that they would be more ready and eager to comply with its stipulations. They could not otherwise fulfil the world mission for which God had chosen them.

In those days there were many Gentiles on the fringe of Judaism, who were believers in the One God, had abandoned idolatry, and attended worship in the Jewish synagogues. They were not required to become Jews, but expected to observe the Divine Law for all mankind, the so-called Laws of Noah. The Apostolic Council gave its verdict to Paul. His Gentile believers in Jesus as Messiah would be accepted as 'Proselytes of the Gate' provided they accepted the Laws of Noah (see *Acts* xv), and given in this respect the status of brethren, without qualifying as Israelites. The verdict was set down in an Official Communication and two members of the Council, who were at any rate trustworthy persons, Judas and Silas, were deputed to convey it to Antioch in association with Paul and Barnabas. The Gentile believers in Jesus, we are told, "rejoiced for the consolation" (*Acts* xv. 31). But not so Paul.

From that time Paul determined to go his own way, repudiating the authority of the Apostolic Council. He regarded their decision, as is evident from his letters, as putting a restriction on the acquisition of converts. His letters show him arguing, sometimes in a rabbinical manner, that by simple faith in the Messianic king of Israel all non-Jews were automatically entitled to Israelite status. Again, here was no question of a new religion.

The whole controversy was not about religious doctrine but about naturalization. In his letter *To the Believers at Rome* Paul claimed that believing Gentiles, as wild olive branches, had been grafted into the olive tree of Israel and become part of Israel (*Rom*. xi). To the *Ephesians* Paul wrote even more plainly:

> Wherefore remember, that ye *were in time past* Gentiles in the flesh, who are called 'uncircumcision' by that which is called 'the circumcision'... that at that time ye were without the Messiah, being aliens from the Commonwealth of Israel, and strangers from the covenants of promise... But now in Messiah Jesus ye who sometimes were far off are *made nigh* by Messiah's blood. For he is our peace, who hath made both one, and hath broken down the Middle Wall of Partition between us... Now therefore ye are no more strangers and foreigners..." (*Eph*. ii. 11-14, 19).

The Middle Wall of Partition was the barrier in the Temple which separated the Court of the Gentiles from the inner Court of Israel. The barrier carried notices in Hebrew, Greek and Latin, warning foreigners that they must not pass beyond it on pain of death. So Paul's view is quite clear. All Gentiles who have acknowledged Jesus as their sovereign lord are now part of Israel. They are one with the People of God. Again there is no hint either of a new religion or of a substitute People of God who are not Jews. God could not be accused, as it were, of 'swapping horses in mid-stream'.

Had either the Apostolic or the Pauline view prevailed there might have been no development of Christian antisemitism, many passages in the New Testament documents would never have been penned, and the evolution of Christianity as a hybrid paganised faith would possibly never have occurred. Responsibility for the transformation has largely to rest on the failure of the Jewish Revolt from Roman domination. All the world was saying in the words of the *Apocalypse of John* (xiii. 4), "Who is like unto the Beast? Who is able to make war with him?"

Christians, if they follow their own scriptures without evasion, can reach only one conclusion, that they are part of the people of Israel nationally.

# 18

# The Times of the Gentiles

We need to be very clear about the transformation that took place between AD 50 and 150 because it was in this period that the Jewish people lost their political status as a nation but survived as a religion. The Romans had always acknowledged the Jewish faith, and indeed had shown great respect for it. There was no general persecution of the Jews in the Roman Empire, in spite of two Jewish revolts from Roman rule. But there was persecution of Messianism, which represented the prophetic and patriotic convictions of the Jewish people, and which the Romans rightly saw as a menace to their empire.

The followers of Jesus were seen as the non-militant, but none the less extremely dangerous aspect of this Messianic menace, more especially as they were missionary, converting to their ideology substantial numbers of non-Jews all over the Empire, especially the slave population disaffected and eager for freedom. The Pauline preachers offered them freedom in Christ, without money and without price. There was nothing to pay for any entrance into the exciting Mysteries of the Messiah, with its promises of future World Government and personal redemption.

When the Christians, after the First Jewish Revolt, severed themselves from the Jews, they hoped that this might allow them to receive acknowledgement as a religion which abjured militancy. But in this they were to be disappointed. The Romans were well aware of what the Messianic was about, and indeed in the East were seeking to arrest members of the family to which Jesus belonged as members of the Jewish royal house, and therefore a potential threat. Among those interrogated, we are told by the Christian historian Eusebius, were two grandchildren of Jude the brother of Jesus.

By this time, towards the close of the first century AD the bulk of the followers of Jesus were of Gentile origin, largely Greeks with antisemitic inclinations. Once therefore Jerusalem had ceased to be the centre of Christian authority, and the Jewish followers of Jesus had been scattered or destroyed, there was less and less inclination to retain a relationship either with the Jews or Judaism. A Christian religion began to be formulated, which varied in its aspects, and indeed in what knowledge it had of the historical Jesus, in the different lands of the Roman empire where Christian communities had been formed. This religion, very naturally, was coloured by the pagan backgrounds of its adherents. In some countries it became more adapted to local traditional religious beliefs than in others. It had to wait until well into the second century before there were serious efforts to formulate a common Christian Faith. One unfortunate effect of this was to transfer the spiritual home of Christianity from Jerusalem to Rome, where both Peter and Paul were executed.

At the close of the Apostolic Age there were a number of versions of Christianity in existence as people joined in different countries and backgrounds, and at this time there was no clear centre of spiritual authority. Christians in Egypt inclined towards Docetism, the view that Jesus as divine only seemed to be human, and to have suffered and died on a cross. Gnosticism was also favoured, converting Christianity into a mystery religion with a relationship with the then popular Hermeticism. It largely lost touch with the historical Jesus.

In Greece, especially at Ephesus in Asia Minor, there was a version of Christianity which favoured the magical and cosmological. Pliny the younger, when Governor of Bithynia, in a letter to the Emperor Trajan, stated that he had learnt from interrogating Christians, "that they met on a fixed day before it was light and sang an antiphonal chant to Christ, as to a god". This could have been the hymn with which *The Gospel of John* opens (see Schonfield, *The Original New Testament*).

In this phase of a Gentilised Christianity there was a virtual repudiation of the Jewish and the Messianic. Christ became a god-name.

In some areas the repudiation of the Law of Moses created what is called antinomianism, which frequently, especially with much slave membership of Christian communities, led to sexual licence at the *Agape*, Christian love-feasts. We have only to read Chapter Two of the *Second Epistle of Peter*, the *Epistle of Jude*, and the Letters to the Seven Churches in the *Revelation*. To a certain extent these developments were a reaction to the earlier prophetic and political Messianism which saw its expectations doomed by Rome's military triumphs. As we have seen, "All the world wondered after the Beast... saying, 'Who is like unto the Beast? Who is able to make war with him?'" (*Rev.* xiii. 3-4).

Christianity would never have come into existence as a coherent religion if an effort had not been made in the second century to create a relationship between the scattered and diverse communities and to promote a new moral and spiritual orthodoxy.

One of the first steps in a long drawn out process was to seek for and assemble the surviving letters of Paul, written to various communities. This was followed by the selection of four out of a number of Gospels, representing the north, south, east and west of the Roman empire, as authorities on Jesus which had respectable antecedents.

Such activities necessarily involved, so far as this was now practicable, historical researches into Christian origins carried out by individuals like Hegesippus, in order to try to form a coherent account of developments. These investigations also revived the sense of the Messianic to an appreciable extent, and called for renewed contact with the Jews, both for information and as a missionary activity. Of existing Jewish sources of information the most prized, as available in Greek, were the historical works of Josephus and the voluminous disquisitions of Philo of Alexandria. But Jewish apocalyptic writings were also utilised.

The breach between the new Christian religion and its Jewish antecedents was now too wide, however, for any reconciliation. Because of its alien membership and pagan slant Christianity regarded itself as having replaced the Jews in God's favour. The story of Jesus was interpreted to convey this. In the succeeding centuries, under Greek and Roman influences, and once Christianity could exert political power, Jew hatred would become the norm.

It was the Eastern Roman empire of the Emperor Constantine and his successors which put the finishing touches to the paganising of Christianity. Constantine had believed it politic, so as to consolidate his authority, to enlist Christian support. The faith long persecuted was now embraced and given official imperial status. The semblance of a Christian history was penned by Eusebius of Caesarea in ten books, and archaeological researches were carried out in the Holy Land, and especially Jerusalem, to recover Christian sites and remains. Helena, mother of Constantine, was devoted to this endeavour.

Now came the time of the Christian Councils which determined what in expressions of the Christian Faith was orthodox and what was heretical. God was finally determined to be a Trinity in language more appropriate to Euclid than to Jesus. There was resistance, by such men as Arius and Nestorius, who would gain a considerable following, but had no hope of suppressing the official creeds. Now for the first time the mother of Jesus became a goddess like the Egyptian Isis, mother of Horus.

Little was now left either of the Messianic, or of the 'religion' of Jesus, and there was a stimulation by the Church of Jew-hatred. Constantine decreed: "We desire to have nothing in common with this so hated people, for the Redeemer has marked out another path for us. To this we will keep, and be free from disgraceful association with this people."

There was desecration and burning of synagogues. The rabbis in Israel had tried to preserve Judaism by retreating within the walls of a new Temple, the *Talmud*. Here the interpretation and commentaries of the *Mishnah* and *Gemara* provided an endless internal engagement, which offset the sufferings of the external world. But this had to be transferred almost entirely to Babylonia, to Sura and Pumbeditha. For Israel too the Messianic was beginning to become more of a dream than a hope, after the failure of Bar-Cochba. Akiba, one of the greatest rabbis, was told by his colleagues that grass would sprout from his chin, and still the Messiah would not have come.

As I have pointed out, for the Church also the Messianic character and function of Jesus had almost disappeared. Instead, increasingly, an ornate religious ceremonialism took over, with a priesthood which became devoted to robes and rituals. The annual Passover service of Israel, as celebrated by Jesus as an orthodox Jew, was converted into the magic of the Mass, in which wafers and wine supposedly turned into his body and blood. It was all very impressive, but utterly alien. The Roman instrument of torture on which this acclaimed 'king of the Jews' had suffered, became a vertical and horizontal gesture and symbol dominating Christian faith and worship in a manner representative of superstition rather than religion.

The populous heaven of the pagan world could not be ignored: it was too dear and too ingrained with the populace. The Church found a means of exchange by substituting male and female saints for gods and goddesses, whose favours could be sought by prayer. The exchange was not difficult. Missionaries to heathen countries aimed at the rulers, who when 'converted' could order all their subjects to embrace Christianity, having only the vaguest notions about it. Some Roman Catholic authorities have now admitted this.

Thus Christianity spread across Europe and into Africa and Asia, and if it had not been checked this would have been the end of Messianism for all time. Judaism could not stem the tide: it had retired from its external impact into its shell, seeking self-preservation rather than conversion of the Gentiles, which would advance the coming of the Kingdom of God on Earth.

It was needed, if the Messianic Hope was to endure, that descendants of the elder son of Abraham should intervene. In the seventh century, like a hot wind from the deserts of Arabia, came the adherents of Islam, sweeping across North Africa and into Europe. Christian idolatry was challenged by a faith which restored the worship of One God, invisible, immaterial and indivisible.

# 19

# Christ as Antichrist

The intervention of Islam was timely, but it was only partially successful. For a thousand years the 'king of the Jews' would be seen to be the archenemy of the Jews, since those who claimed to represent him would persecute them in his name. The greater part of the Christian clergy in Europe were either the instigators or promoters of a programme to kill or convert the Jews in Christianised lands. Nearly all Christians of today are almost entirely ignorant of the crimes committed against the Jews in the name of Jesus. It is right, therefore, that they should be confronted with the facts.

In the West under the Gothic monarchs the compulsory conversion of the Jews began in earnest. A decree of King Sisebuto in 614 reads in part as follows:

> Wherefore, if any of those Jews as yet unbaptized, shall delay to be himself baptized, or neglect to send his children and slaves to the priest for baptism while it is offered, thus abiding without the grace of baptism, for the space of one year from the issue of this decree: every such transgressor, wherever found, shall be stripped, and shall suffer one hundred lashes, as likewise the due penalty of exile: his goods shall be forfeit to the king; and in order that his life may be the more painful, such goods shall become the perpetual property of those on whom the king shall bestow them. (See the Spanish Code *Fuero Juzgo*.)

Those who submitted to compulsory conversion, very largely continued to be crypto-Jews, against whom the Fourth Church Council of Toledo decreed:

> Many who were formerly exalted to the Christian Faith, are now known not only in blasphemy against Christ to perpetuate Jewish rites, but have even dared to practise the abomination of

circumcision... Transgressors after this sort, being apprehended by authority of the prelates, shall be recalled to the true worship according to Christian doctrine: so that those whom their own will cannot amend, may be coerced by sacerdotal correction. (*Canon* 59)

We decree that the sons and daughters of Jews are to be separated from their parents, lest they likewise be involved in their errors. (*Canon* 62)

Jews having Christian wives, are to be admonished by the bishop of their diocese, that if they desire to abide with them, they must become Christian; and if, being so admonished, they refuse to obey, they shall be separated. (*Canon* 63)

Jews who were formerly Christians, but are now deniers of the Faith in Christ, are not to be admitted to evidence at law, although they declare themselves Christians. (*Canon* 64)

To quote from my own studies: "Can testimony be clearer as to what was the aim of these enactments? Judaism and the very name of Jew was an abomination, and must be rooted out of any Christian country. If Christ was incarnate anywhere, surely it was in the souls of those who stoutly resisted him. But perhaps it was not Christ, but another in the shape of the outraged Nazarene."

Mercifully for the Jews of Europe there came a brief interval of peace, which they were not again to enjoy for several centuries. The breath of the old-wise East blew into the West, bearing learning and enlightenment, and with wisdom came a measure of toleration. Temporarily a golden age dawned for Judaism, to which the liberal Carlovingian kings greatly contributed. Pepin, Charlemagne and Louis le Debonnaire eased the Jewish burden, so that the populace began to regard the former outcasts again as "the only people of God". Charlemagne chose a Jew named Isaac as one of his ambassadors to the Court of the famous Caliph, Haroun al-Raschid. Louis, in turn, had as one of his confidential advisers the Jewish physician Zededkiah.

As one outcome it was permitted to Jews to engage in disputations with Christians without fear of death or suffering. A notable one of these was promoted by the Dominicans and held in Barcelona from July 20 – 24, 1263. The debate was on the themes (1) Whether the Messiah has appeared, (2) Whether the Messiah announced by the Prophets was to be considered as a god, or as a man born of human parents, (3) Whether the Jews or Christians are in possession of the True Faith. On the Jewish side was the famous Rabbi Nahmanides, who left a record of the proceedings.

But such possibilities had largely been offset by the Crusades. Surely one of the strangest anomalies in Christian history was the setting forth of thousands of Christians to deliver the sepulchre of a saviour who had been a Jew with their hands imbued in Jewish blood. A Jewish record of the time reads:

> The abominable Germans and French rose up against them [the Jews], people of a fierce countenance... and they said, 'Let us be revenged for our Messiah upon the Jews that are among us, and let us destroy them from being a nation, that the name of Israel be had no more in remembrance; so shall they change their glory and be like unto us; then will we go to the East.'

The Bishop Engelbert, who received at his palace the wretched Jewish survivors of the massacre of Trèves, greeted them with the words: "Wretches, your sins have come upon you; ye who blasphemed the Son of God and calumniated his Mother. This is the cause of your present miseries, which – if you persist in your obduracy – will destroy you body and soul for ever."

The Roman Catholics could not conceive at all of the Kingdom of God on Earth in terms of the Hebrew Prophets and Jesus himself. They much preferred a new Roman empire, which was an anti-Christian concept. So was born the idea of the Holy Roman Empire. Its philosophy has been set out by Lord Bryce:

> As God, in the midst of his celestial hierarchy, ruled blessed spirits in paradise, so the Pope, his vicar, raised above priests, bishops, metropolitans, reigned over the souls of man below. But as God is Lord of earth as well as of heaven, so must he (the *Imperator coelestis*) be represented by a second earthly viceroy, the Emperor (*Imperator terrenus*), whose authority shall be of and for this present life... It is under the emblem of soul and body that the relation of the papal and imperial power is presented to us throughout the Middle Ages... Thus the Holy Roman Church and the Holy Roman Empire are one and the same thing, in two aspects; and Catholicism, the principle of the universal Christian society, is also Romanism; that is, it rests upon Rome as the origin and type of its universality; manifesting itself in a mystic dualism which corresponds to the two

natures of its founder. As divine and eternal, its head is the Pope, to whom souls have been entrusted; as human and temporal, the emperor, commissioned to rule over men's bodies and acts.

Medieval Christianity could not fail to be anti-Jewish since its goal was a new Roman despotism.

Catholicism, because of its traditional Graeco-Roman antisemitism, could never entertain the Messianic with its non-militant idealism, as idealism represented by the Jewish prophets. The Messianic fore-saw the taming of the wild-beast states by the child Israel, when na-tion would no longer lift up sword against nation, neither shall they learn war any more. And Jesus himself had said, "Unless you become as little children you cannot enter the Kingdom of God."

The advent of Protestantism, with its "back to the Bible" emphasis, brought initially some concern for the plight of the Jews. In a book published in 1523 entitled *Dass Jesus ein geborener Jude gewesen* (That Jesus was by birth a Jew), Martin Luther wrote:

> Those fools the papists, bishops, sophists, monks, have formerly so dealt with the Jews, that every good Christian would rather have been a Jew. And if I had been a Jew, and seen such stupidity and such blockheads reign in the Christian Church, I would rather be a pig than a Christian. They have treated the Jews as if they were dogs, not men, and as if they were fit for nothing but to be reviled. They are blood relations of our Lord; therefore if we respect flesh and blood, the Jews belong to Christ more than we. I beg, therefore, my dear Papists, if you become tired of abusing me as a heretic, that you begin to revile me as a Jew. Therefore, it is by force, treating them deceitfully or ignominiously... we prohibit them from working amongst us, from living and having social intercourse with us, forcing them if they would remain with us to be usurers.

But such blandishments did not attract Jews to reformed Chris-tianity any more than to Roman Catholicism, and Luther changed his tune. Twenty-one years later he published another book *Von den Juden und ihren Lügen* (About the Jews and their Lies). Here he vented his disappointment in very different language. "Doubt not, beloved in Christ, that after the Devil you have no more bitter, ven-omous, violent enemy than the real Jew, the Jew most earnest in his belief." He urged his followers:

(i) Burn their synagogues and schools; what will not burn, bury with earth, that neither stone nor rubbish remain. (ii) In like manner break into and destroy their houses. (iii) Take away all their prayer-books and talmuds, in which are nothing but god-lessness, lies, cursing and swearing. (iv) Forbid their rabbis to teach on pain of life and limb." And so on.

Certainly the immediate result of the Reformation was not materi-ally to lighten the Jewish burden. Abbott, in *Israel in Europe* (p.127), wrote:

Protestant Germany took up the tale of persecution in the sixteenth century where Catholic Germany had left off in the fifteenth. The Jews were given the alternative of baptism or banishment in Berlin, were expelled from Bavaria in 1553, from Brandenburg in 1573, and the tragedy of oppression was carried on through the ensuing centuries.

What the Reformation did achieve was a revived interest in Biblical prediction and Second Adventism, and inevitably this invited con-sideration of the destiny of the Jews. If the Jews were not brought nearer to Christ the Christians were brought nearer to the Hebrew prophets.

# 20
# *A New Awakening*

In many respects in the Middle Ages time had seemed almost to be standing still; but in the fifteenth century a profound acceleration developed which was to transform the human scene. The rigidness was by no means ended, and fought hard against progress. But it was a losing battle. Romanism had its peak with the Emperor Charles V in the sixteenth century. But then Ivan the Terrible of Russia claimed the status of Caesar as Czar, and sought to continue despotism. This, however, was on the fringe of European progress and more akin to the monolithic governmental structures of Asia.

One of the heralds of change had been the introduction of printing in the middle of the fifteenth century; and this, among other things, enabled the Bible to become more widely available. The English King James Version appeared in 1611. The laity could now study its contents for themselves, and make their own interpretations.

The world was now determined to be a globe, a planet circulating round the sun like other planets in our system. We could begin to view our universe through the telescope. Here the names of Copernicus (1473-1543) and Galileo Galilei (1564-1642) are outstanding. These advances stimulated the voyages of discovery. Columbus, seeking Asia in the westward direction, encountered America in 1492. Vasco da Gama rounded Africa to reach India in 1498, and Magellan rounded South America and crossed the Pacific in 1519.

It was a rapid and tremendous development; but with it also there came a feeling of climax. Could it be that the Age would be the end of all the Ages? Men began to seek for signs that the Kingdom of God was at hand, something that Christians had not done with such zeal for fifteen hundred years. The Jews too were affected by such

118

speculations, and hopes that the Messiah was about to come to deliver them were awakened in many Jewish hearts.

And what people sought for they inevitably found. Reading the Bible in the vernacular, but still in a Gentile manner as a book of infallible oracles, there was not only a revolt against Catholic orthodoxy but a conviction that Romanism was pagan and anti-Christian and represented the Antichrist of the Last Times.

Seeking for Signs of the Times became an engagement both for non-Conformist Christians and for Kabbalistic Jews. The Christian sects studied the book of *Revelation*, with its intimations of apostasy, war, plague and famine. The Jews too were affected by the Christian expectations which, because of the book of *Revelation*, attached special significance to the year 1666.

The imminence of the Messianic Age was used by the Rabbi Menasseh ben Israel in a letter to Cromwell and the English parliament to petition for permission for the Jews to be allowed back to England. He pointed out that "the opinions of many Christians and my own do agree herein, that we both believe that the restoring time for our nation into their native land is very near at hand."

At this juncture a claimant to be the Messiah did appear. His name was Shabbethai Zebi, and he was born in Smyrna on the Jewish national fast day the Ninth of Ab, 23 July 1626. Shabbethai was mystically inclined, and was strongly affected by a Kabbalistic passage in the *Zohar* which indicated to many Jews that the Messiah would redeem Israel and restore them to their own land in the year corresponding to 1648.

A great part of Protestant Christendom was now strangely unquiet, filled with Messianic expectations and forebodings of coming Judgment, and this had been working up for some time. The national conversion of the Jewish people no longer appeared as a dim and distant prospect, still less as an unattainable goal. And their redeemed status was in many minds. It was natural that the Jews should be stirred by the rumours and tidings. A century earlier David Reubeni had come to Europe with talk of a Jewish kingdom in the East. Antonio de Montesinos was claiming that the North-American Indians were the Lost Ten Tribes. In England there were rumours that the Jews had offered Cromwell half a million pounds for St.Paul's Cathedral to become their synagogue, and one writer suggested solving the Irish problem by making that country over to them.

It would appear that Shabbethai's response to such tidings, and pressures put upon him by those around, had finally decided him, a youthful mystic, to take the plunge. He was only twenty-two at the time. At Smyrna on the Jewish Day of Atonement he publicly pronounced the sacred four-letter Hebrew name of God YHVH, which in ancient times had been done only by the Jewish High Priest. His associates took this as a sign, and soon evidences were forthcoming from supporters that confirmed that he was indeed the destined Messiah. Especially was pressure put upon him by a certain Nathan of Gaza who met Shabbethai when he was in the Holy Land. Nathan claimed for himself that he was Elijah the Prophet, returned as the Messiah's herald, and it was he who announced that the Messianic Era would begin in 1666. The Messiah would lead the Tribes of Israel back to their own land "riding on a lion with a seven-headed dragon in its jaw".

The "Glad Tidings" had spread swiftly to the West. Jewish merchants in Amsterdam began to close their businesses preparatory to returning to the Land of Israel. Whole communities of Jews got ready to depart. Prayers for "our Lord and King Shabbethai Zebi" were read in some quite orthodox synagogues. Men and women, and even children, fell into prophetic ecstasies.

Even Christians began to wonder what these happenings could portend. Was Shabbethai the real Christ? Was he Antichrist? The wildest rumours were gaining currency. To the north of Scotland a ship had been sighted with sails blazoned with the words "The Twelve Tribes of Israel", manned with sailors who spoke only Hebrew.

On Jewish New Year's Day in 1665 Shabbethai finally took the plunge. At Smyrna, declaring himself to be the Messiah, his announcement was greeted with the blowing of horns in the synagogue amidst cries of "Long live our King and Messiah!"

Christians conveyed the news to Europe, where even men of intelligence were affected. It is on record that the German sage Heinrich Oldenburg wrote to Spinoza (*Epistle 16*), "All the world here is talking of a rumour of the return of the Israelites... to their own country... Should the news be confirmed, it may bring about a revolution in all things."

But the end of all the hopes that had been aroused was to be tragedy. In 1666 Jews in many places had received a circular letter written by Shabbethai's secretary Samuel Primo. It was to this effect:

The first-begotten Son of God, Shabbethai Zebi, Messiah and

Redeemer of the people of Israel, to all the sons of Israel, Peace!
Since ye have been deemed worthy to behold the great day and
the fulfilment of God's Word by the Prophets, your lament and
sorrow must be changed into joy, and your fasting into merri-
ment; for ye shall weep no more. Rejoice with song and melody,
and change the day formerly spent in sadness and sorrow into a
day of jubilee, because I have appeared.

But all too soon there was to be a great shock for Jewish believers.
Shabbethai had been pressed to fulfil the prediction that he should
take the crown from the head of the Turkish Sultan, and he set out
for Constantinople. But he was betrayed, and was taken to Adrianople,
where confronted with the alternative of conversion to Islam or death
he accepted advice to choose the former. Brought before the Sultan
he put a Turkish turban on his own head (16 Sept. 1666). He was
rewarded with the title of Effendi, and presently declared in a letter
to his followers at Smyrna: "God has made me an Ishmaelite. He
commanded, and it was done. The ninth day of my regeneration."
Ultimately he died in Albania.

What did all these circumstances convey? Did they mean that the
whole Messianic business, both Christian and Jewish, was a snare and
delusion, a chimera? It might give this impression. But there could
be another interpretation, that the march of discovery and scientific
progress had brought the Messianic process back to life again, even
if it had been in an unfortunate and credulous way. The forward
movement of mankind could not fundamentally be separated from
the Messianic Hope; for this conveyed that there was a goal and a
destiny for mankind to be accomplished. In other periods of history
we can find a similar conjunction, a static condition abruptly converted into a dynamic as a result of scientific discoveries, natural
catastrophes, and political and spiritual upheavals.

There would seem to be a lesson which mankind needs to learn,
that the progress of mankind is inextricably bound up with Israel and
with individuals sprung from Israel. They represent both the stimu-
lating energy in human affairs and the ultimate goal to which it is
directed.

## 21

# *Acceleration*

The Messianic Process was to be greatly speeded up in the seventeenth to nineteenth centuries. The life of our planet would become almost completely transformed by advances in many fields, and this activity would continue into the twentieth century and beyond.

First of all our physical Earth would be revealed to an extent never practicable previously. Extensive territories in Asia, Africa and the Americas hitherto labelled *Terra Incognita* were progressively penetrated by intrepid explorers, some of them in the interests of spreading the Word of God, others in the cause of science. In due course even the North and South Poles would be reached. The stories of these achievements still make exciting reading. And then there were parts of Australia to discover.

Both our world and its contents became increasingly disclosed. The flora and fauna in all their diversities, and many diverse expressions of our common humanity, could be revealed, described and recorded. One consequence, through the slave trade and colonialism, would be a spreading round the globe of various races, white, black, red, yellow and brown, with their cultures; and these would in due course begin to mingle. The flora and fauna of the planet would be universalized by the creation of botanical and zoological gardens, and human needs would be served by new drugs and foods. For the first time the foundations were being laid for a whole world outlook with the potentiality for ultimate world unification.

But now too there could be an effective beginning of reading the riddle of the Earth's past. Man could travel back in time as well as forward, studying geology, fossils and skeletal remains. It was a shock to begin to learn of the profound antiquity of our planet, of types of vegetation and creatures which had flourished and become extinct in very remote ages. One outcome would be Darwin's theory of evolution.

Just as thrilling, and even more positively accessible, was the capacity to acquire knowledge of a much more recent past, the beginning and development of civilized human history. The frontiers of archaeology were now being greatly extended, and little by little there emerged the images in graphic detail of long extinct cultures and civilizations, particularly initially those of the biblical powers of Egypt, Assyria and Babylonia.

The physical remains were dramatically supplemented by the capacity to read the dead languages of the Bible lands. Napoleon was to invade Egypt taking with him a number of savants. There was the discovery of a bilingual inscription in Greek and ancient Egyptian, the Rosetta Stone, which revealed the secret of the mysterious hiero-glyphics. It is a well-known story. In the Greek text were read the names of Ptolemy and Cleopatra, and in corresponding positions in the native version were symbols enclosed in cartridge-like outlines (in French *cartouches*), representing these names. The wedge-like (cuneiform) writing of ancient Mesopotamia was in its turn inter-preted, revealing the history of the lands from which Abraham had sprung. We could now be in contact with the Pharaohs of the Oppression of Israel and the Exodus, and could compare the Law of Moses with the Code of Hammurabi. The Bible was coming to light in a manner which previously would have been thought impossible. There was also opening up the possibility of a much more detailed and reliable chronology of the Past.

Christians were naturally very enthusiastic about the exploration of Bible lands, which threw so much light on the Bible itself. But this activity inevitably raised questions of how reliable factually the Bible was. It could now be examined with a freedom which previously would have been deemed blasphemous.

There was room now not just for consideration of the Bible as the Word of God, the text book of religion, but as a collection of ancient documents whose origins required investigation and their reliability testing. Man's theology could begin to take second place, and God's anthropology the first place. This would help, notably in Germany, to release Biblical interpretation from servitude to texts. At the same time the overall picture of a purpose and objective in Man's existence on our Earth could more readily be apprehended. And this would have major social consequences, namely, that all men are free and equal.

Sects like the Levellers had arrived at this conviction. There was the slogan, "When Adam delved and Eve span, who was then the gentleman?" The Rights of Man became something to strive for in a world of ancient class distinctions. The right to rule of an aristocracy by virtue of blood and family was being increasingly and sometimes violently rejected, as in the French Revolution, and at the other end of the scale the right to convert humans, largely Negroes, into slaves, which led to the American War between the North and South. The rejections were a consequence of Nonconformist Christianity, which had been developing both a missionary zeal and a social conscience.

This Christianity was very conscious of what were believed to be the Signs of the Times heralding the Second Advent of Christ, and eager therefore "to preach the Gospel to every creature". And this particularly included the Jews, who now progressively were being given permission to return to countries from which they had been excluded. They were often denied the full rights of citizens; but they were more tolerated and not a little envied as members of the People of God, destined to play an important role in the coming Millennium.

Shakespeare had had understanding of the plight of the Jew and the Negro in his creations of Shylock and Othello; but now there was an intrusion of the Messianic in Oratorio like Handel's *Judas Maccabaeus* and more notably *Messiah*, with its peak in the Hallelujah Chorus. The aim of the advent of the Kingdom of God on Earth chimed with a sense of social mission in the Son, which foresaw the building of Jerusalem in England's green and pleasant land.

The Jews, who for centuries had had restricted opportunities for self-expression, would respond with a long list of great musical composers and performers. And in his turn the emancipated Negro would contribute in musical sound, song and dance, to the spiritualising of the Machine Age with its undercurrent of suffering.

The moral and social teachings of the Bible were now able to have an effect they had never had before in Western public life and policy. Not only was there being exhibited in many connections a genuine social concern, there was also the apprehension by the masses that they had equal rights with those who were better off and they were entitled to claim them and challenge exploitation. With the coming of the Machine Age with its factory life a working class movement blossomed and achieved power with the trades unions to improve conditions. Very appropriately, the movement functioned through 'chapels'.

In industrial centres the gas, the fog and the smoke and the grime were depriving life of beauty and comfort. Millions existed under conditions of great misery and squalor, so that there was a tremendous need for amelioration. In England these conditions would be reflected in the novels of Dickens, and in more direct writings which stirred the social conscience, especially of the new middle class. To speak of Britain in particular, there was a response of numerous social welfare agencies, many of them religiously motivated. There was the Salvation Army sponsored by the Booth family. There were the Boys' Brigade, the Ragged Schools, societies for widows and orphans, hospitals and hostelries.

The middle class itself was a product of the Industrial Revolution, which built up the manufacture and distribution of goods and services, which previously had been reflected in the farmers and small tradesmen. Productive power had been intensified by machinery, and this also improved the quality of life for the masses.

Food and drink from remote places were within the reach of multitudes. Once it had been those like Queen Anne who "sometimes counsel took, and sometimes tay". Now there was widespread enjoyment of tea, coffee and cocoa, and the commodities of other lands. This development was greatly accelerated by the employment of steam in locomotion. The world became much smaller and the quality of life much richer with the arrival of the train and the steamship and the balloon. People and goods could be moved around much more readily, and this would have a profound effect on foreign relationships.

But also engines of war, and the coming of the iron-clad battleship and eventually the submarine, made international conflict more lethal. One outcome was the Geneva Conventions and the institution of the International Red Cross by Henri Dunant. The idea of international law as essential for civilized society had been stressed by Hugo Grotius in his work *De Jure Belli ac Pacis* in the seventeenth century as an outcome of the Thirty Years' War (1618-48). Such 'law', at the end of the nineteenth century was becoming imperative, and this was reflected in The Hague Conferences of 1899 and 1907. In international disputes there was recognised the need for uninvolved countries to act as mediators, and the principle of arbitration was embodied in the setting up of a permanent court at The Hague for this purpose.

Some would believe, however, that "government by the people, for the people" was an essential condition for the coming of world peace. The common people were in a common peril of exploitation. They had no animosity for each other, only for the boss class which ran human affairs. Under communism a new era for mankind would begin. In their manifesto of 1848 Marx and Engels sent out their clarion call, "Working men of all countries unite!" Time would show that communism would prove just as imperialist as Romanism. Czarist Russia was the land where communism would find conditions congenial to its implementation.

That same Czarist Russia, however, was contributing to another development. The *pogroms*, with the massacres of Jews, were responsible for a widespread emigration which helped to people the New World, especially the United States, with many Jewish citizens, who would have an effect on its later policies. More apocalyptically the *pogroms* promoted a Jewish sense that Jews could never be free from persecution except in their own land. There was the *Chovevi Zion* (Lovers of Zion) movement, and more dramatically and consequentially the Zionism of Theodor Herzl, author of *Alt Neuland* (Old New Land). Herzl put it to World Jewry, "If you *will* it, it is no dream."

Jews had not acted together for many centuries, and they found it very difficult to do so now. Zionism, however, did have a strong appeal to Protestant Christians, who saw in it a Sign of the Times, and consequently gave it moral support and encouragement. On the eve of two thousand years since the birth of Jesus the Messiah the era of restoration of God's ancient people seemed now imminent, and this could have only one meaning that Jesus would be back in the world once more "to set up a kingdom that would never be destroyed".

Coinciding with these developments was a veritable spate of recovery of ancient Jewish and ancient Christian books and records, some by exploration, especially of Near Eastern monastic libraries, and some by chance. The finds, and others which would follow in the twentieth century, would put the clock back some two thousand years, in fresh capacity to comprehend how Christianity had begun, and how alien it had been to what it would become later. The New Testament no longer stood monumentally alone: it stood in the midst of records which could more accurately interpret it.

# 22
# *War and Peace*

We are now in the twentieth century, and as I write we are nearing its close. It has been very much *my* century, since I was born within a few months of its commencement and I have participated in many aspects of its development. These developments have exhibited a speeding-up process unprecedented in human history, exceeding the major acceleration of the previous period. Chiefly it has been a century in which there has been a progressive change of emphasis from 'international' to 'world'.

Already, near the beginning of the century, our planet had been explored to an extent that had brought cognisance of almost every part of it. There had also been mechanical advances which would speed communication by land and sea, and under the sea by submarine. But the chief advance would be the progressive conquest of the air. First the aeroplane arrived on the scene, and as a boy I was myself able to witness the exploit of Blériot in flying across the English Channel. In a few decades our planet would be criss-crossed with a network of air lines carrying millions at great speeds to every part of the globe.

Latterly, with the employment of the rocket, man would reach and set foot on the moon, create space stations, and even send responsive instruments throughout the solar system. The progress was awesome, and the pictures taken thrilling for the human race. The "one step for man" landing on the moon's surface was indeed a tremendous advance for mankind, and as an experience it was almost matched by the God's-eye view of Mother Earth now obtainable and the venturing out of individuals into the vastness of space.

Cinematography and later television arrived to make major human events come alive, so that they could be viewed by millions as if they had been on the spot. The reporting of history had acquired a new dimension, and also a perpetuation more precise than human memory, and the sense of participation could arouse emotion over distant happenings as if they had taken place in the next street. Overnight, as it seemed, both the globe and our solar system had undergone a tremendous contraction: but also our human responsibilities had profoundly increased. Who our neighbour was could no longer mean the man next door or even our fellow-countryman. He represented the human race. We were on the eve of a society that conferred on all of us a planetary responsibility for care and concern.

But that sense of responsibility would not come about easily in view of self-interest and power-seeking, more especially by those governments with authoritarian ideologies. The advances of science could be put to destructive use on an unprecedented scale, so that by the end of the century they would constitute a threat to all life on our planet. Poison gas and atomic weapons were conceptions in the human mind before they became facts of life.

By the commencement of the First World War (1914-18) we already had the iron-clad battleship and the submarine, and we would go on to have the machine-gun, the bomber, and the tank. We were acquiring a destructive God-power rather than one of love. As Kipling put it in his poem *M'Andrew's Hymn*:

What I ha' seen since ocean-steam began
Leaves me na doot for the machine: but what about the man?
The man that counts, wi' all his runs, one million mile o' sea:
Four time the span from earth to moon... How far, O Lord,
    from Thee?

The movements for world peace at the dawn of the century were all too soon to be frustrated by aggressive imperialism, and we would be plunged into a conflict that seemed to fulfil all the Biblical anticipations of the Last Times. Students of prophecy were not slow to label the war with the dread name of Armageddon, and to draw the conclusion that the Second Advent of Christ must be imminent. As a preliminary the Four Horsemen of the Apocalypse (War, Plague, Famine and Death) had been let loose on mankind.

For the threatened Western Allies this was a Holy War, and in proof divine manifestations were called upon, such as the Angels of Mons. In the other camp the Ottoman Empire was allied with Germany, and this would lead to the British and French invading

128

Palestine. General Allenby was the British commander, and it did not take long for his name to be defined in Arabic as *Allah Nebi* (Prophet of God).

With the British forces in the Middle East were two battalions of the Royal Fusiliers composed of Jewish volunteers; one of them was my elder brother Leslie. And these battalions had been recruited by my father Major William Schonfield. Jestingly they were described as the Jewsiliers, with the regimental motto "No Advance without Security". As a boy I met a number of them, and was greatly impressed by their love for the ancient Jewish homeland, the land of Israel. I was also present at the great London gathering in celebration of the famous Balfour Declaration by the British government in favour of again making Palestine a national home for the Jewish people.

These circumstances added very considerably to Christian conviction that the Last Times before the Second Advent had now come. I discovered this when as a school-leaver I went on land work, and had as companions some conscientious objectors of the sect of Christadelphians. We had many discussions, and for the first time I read the New Testament, a copy of which I had borrowed from my landlady.

All kinds of ideas were in circulation at this time. One of them was that the chronology of the Last Times had been precisely predicted in measurement of the passages in the Great Pyramid of Egypt. But the readings of the sign were in vain. Jesus did not return. Could it be that the Messianic Hope, as the Christians understood it, was much too literal in what it seemed to promise? Because of our literal-mindedness we could have got things all wrong, and failed to perceive what it is essential for us to grasp. On the other hand, by the general rejection of the Messianic as an indispensable process, we could be defeating our future by conceiving unrealistic means and unworkable methods of salvation.

This seemed to be the case at the end of the First World War. As a means of maintaining peace in the future the League of Nations was created. It had much to commend it, chiefly in bonding a secretariat, and a body of individuals, for functioning in a world context for the common good. It also instituted an international parliament where matters of dispute, as well as common needs, could be debated and resolved without resort to open conflict and disastrous war.

The First World War had shown that the conventions of the permanent Court of Arbitration at The Hague were not enough to check militancy. It had been stipulated (Article 3) that: "The right of tendering good offices, or mediation, belongs to the Powers who are strangers to the dispute, even during the progress of hostilities. The exercise of this right can never be considered, by either of the litigant parties, as an unfriendly act." But this could not check the wilful resort to force of individual Powers, or alliances of Powers, to seek domination or to fulfil their own ambitions.

It did not take many years for the advent of ideologies to constitute a new threat to peace. These would invest the idea of the State with the ruthlessness of the age of power, while claiming an authorization of the spirit. There was Fascism, Nazism, and – in the East – State Shintoism, all reminiscent of an antique Romanism. The League of Nations could not cope with these developments, which in Europe brought death to some six million Jews. Once again anti-Jewish was also anti-Messianic. For the Nazis "Christ was but a Jewish pig." The Second World War was let loose in 1939, but it could not be claimed again that this was Armageddon, though it would end with the horror of the atomic bombs dropped on Hiroshima and Nagasaki.

It was not with any true vision of peace that the United Nations would be created, but as the League "with teeth in it". The Four Powers of Britain, China, the Soviet Union and the United States, would act as "guarantors of international peace and security pending the re-establishment of law and order and the inauguration of a system of general security" (Moscow Declaration of October 1943). That system could never materialize on such a basis, and it would not take long for the United Nations to be disregarded in Great Power relationships, even though it had many additional members all over the world in States which formerly had been Colonies.

The idea of an International Police Force was tried, but could not cope with States that insisted that they were a law to themselves. And there were alliances like the British Commonwealth, the Communist Bloc, and the European Community, which did achieve considerable success because of common interests.

But a world at peace, especially in view of the advance of destructive power, demanded a universalism for which there were no indications of a general readiness. What many States were seeking was to establish a secure place for themselves in the scheme of things, both politically and commercially, which would give them a strong position when it came to bargaining over the shape of things to come.

No great progress could be made until in all thinking about the future the word 'world' could effectively be substituted for the word 'international'. For this the sovereign States were far from prepared; and indeed it was a concept to which they were constitutionally alien. One could use the word world legitimately only in a geographical and scientific sense, or as a generalization. It was only individuals who had the mental agility to recognise that somehow the world must unite or perish; and all too often even they were imagining an association of a familiar kind, a world federal government.

The Brotherhood of Man in a World context was fundamentally a Messianic concept. As far back as 1776 Granville Sharp had declared: "Under the glorious dispensation of the Gospel we are absolutely bound to consider ourselves as citizens of the world." Similarly, after the First World War a Persian Christian, Yervant H. Iskender, had stressed that, "An all-embracing unity is thus the solution of the problem of putting an end to war for ever... The world's inhabitants must, under one inspiring name – 'the citizens of the world' – unite to put an end to war." One of the Nazi complaints against the Jews was that they were not motivated by "blood and soil" but by world citizenship.

It was almost inevitable, therefore, that the circumstances bringing about the Second World War and its aftermath should again emphasize the Messianic One World viewpoint with Jews as its advocates. One of them was the American ex-bomber pilot, Garry Davis, whose exploits in crossing frontiers without a passport gave rise to the Paris-based International Registry of World Citizens, and who told his story in a book entitled *My Country is the World*. Another's initiative was my own.

On the eve of the outbreak of World War II I had had a vision of a new nation composed exclusively of world citizens, which would pioneer the way towards a united world by its services and example. It would act in the mediatorial and exemplary character that the ideal Israel was meant to act, and thus pave the way for a world unity of the future for which mankind was still far from ready. I have related the circumstances and the thinking behind them in my own book *The Politics of God*. The new nation was named the Mondcivitan Republic (Commonwealth of World Citizens). It was proclaimed in being publicly at a Constituent Assembly of its initial citizens from

131

many lands at the Temple of Peace and Health at Cardiff, Wales, which was also the headquarters in Wales of the United Nations Association. Diplomatic personalities from East and West were present as observers, and the proceedings were televised. This was in August 1956. By 1959 the infant Servant-Nation of Mankind had carried out world-wide general elections, and by courtesy of the government of Austria, its first parliament was convened in Vienna in May of that year.

The Mondcivitan Republic as the Pioneer People, the advance guard of a united world, which anyone of any race, colour or creed could apply to join, had a freedom to take initiatives in a way no sovereign state could do, since it had no partisanship and was not tied to any territory. As first president I had the chief responsibility for these. One of them is still very pertinent. This was in connection with the dangers of fall-out resulting from the testing of nuclear weapons, and was sent to the member states of NATO and the Warsaw Pact in September 1961 under the title "An Urgent Call On Behalf Of Humanity". I quote here from the text:

> The Mondcivitan Republic... asserts as an incontrovertible fact that no government in the world has been invested with a mandate which permits it to exercise, or attempt to exercise, the power of life and death over any peoples... This not only excludes all acts of coercion and aggression involving the people of any country or countries, but any action, such as the testing of nuclear or other weapons, which may be a danger to them or inflict injury upon them.

The outcome was that resolutions were adopted in October and November of that year by the General Assembly of the United Nations couched in similar language. For this, and other interventions of a peace-making nature, one of them a factor in resolving the Cuban Crisis of 1962, I was nominated for the Nobel Peace Prize.

# 23

# *What We Now Face*

We are now at the beginning of an age unprecedented in human history, and one which has in store both potentialities and problems no previous generation has ever been required to meet. In certain respects we are now becoming gods, while exhibiting qualities far more degrading than those we ascribe to beasts. How then can this be deemed a time when the Messianic goal of heaven on earth would have its fulfilment? If we are realistic we must accept that mankind has a long way to go yet. Certain advances are accelerating greatly, but we do not have a God-sense of time. Nor do we know whether, before we can advance much further, we may have to face a prolonged standstill, or even a period of retreat to very near zero. Long before Man appeared on the earth it took vast ages for creatures to transfer from water to dry land, and meet with setbacks which took ages to surmount.

Yes, we can be proud of our creative capacity, the machines and the instruments we are devising with competencies much greater than our own, except in moral judgments, in having all that we mean by a soul. We can already see that our creations can do things much faster and better than we can; and to an extent we have appreciated that in these respects increasingly a growing world population is irrevocably being deprived of employment. For many millions it will hold good that "the Devil has work for idle hands to do." Soon these millions could constitute the majority of the human race, and by thwarting them of working rights their human dignity will become degraded, and they could revert to a savagery intensified by access to all the advancing mechanical means of destruction. Politicians, in their power-seeking to capture votes, are refusing to face up to this reality, and pretend that unemployment can be mastered without a return to a less mechanised life style. They have devised no desirable functions for the out-of-work to be engaged in that represents a dignified and desirable vocation.

But worse than this, the more Man puts himself at the service of the machine, as the slave of its character and needs, the more soulless does Man become. This is already evident as we near the close of the present century. In commerce and in government the machine is called upon to take over responsibility. Human beings don't deal with other human beings in a human manner, with feeling and concern. Relationships become more and more mechanical, and automatic, evading taking decisions or instituting a personal inquiry into grievances. In this respect in many industries, and in national and municipal contexts, the staff at all levels have become mechanical spokesmen. On some occasions there is outcry at decisions which are unethical or exhibit a lack of humanity; but they are not sufficiently heeded. And ignoring grievances, or unfeelingly putting people off, is everywhere on the increase.

The deprived classes are everywhere on the way to becoming the depraved classes, resorting to all kinds of actions to give life excitement and objectivity. And who can blame them?

The alternatives would seem to be clear. Either we greatly enlarge the area and the variety of concerns in which man operates in an orderly manner, so as to absorb the working population of our planet, or we must very greatly reduce the number of individuals for whom we have to make provision. If we favour the latter this would be a sign that mankind is accepting defeat, that the machine will have the last word. We would be at the beginning of a second creation, with the machine having to evolve into a new humanity by progressively acquiring a soul.

Present indications are uncertain, but incline towards curbing population growth. This is being achieved by enlisting the services of the Four Horsemen of the Apocalypse. Wars, revolutions, ideological rivalries, and anarchic murders, are engaging in orgies of killing with the weapons of destruction now so readily available. Millions are dying of starvation. Fatal accidents have been multiplied through mechanical and atomic devices. And homosexuality and birth control have been making their assault on population growth. There has been an increase in suicides. Life is now held cheaper than at any previous period.

If conflict was to bring about another world war, the chances are

– as it is now widely recognised – that this could spell the doom of civilized society as we have known it.

But there are also more favourable signs, signs that involve feeling and selflessness. In many connections the spirit of disinterested service manifests itself, in the battle with suffering and disease, care for the aged and infirm, famine relief, labour in the cause of peace, and so on.

We are in the midst of what the ancient Essenes, whose literature we have recovered, described as the war between the Children of Light and the Children of Darkness. It lies within the power of the Children of Light to become victorious. And this applies to many critical periods, of the future as of the past. And it is where the Messianic has to come into our calculations.

The Messianic has always argued that we humans are on this planet not by accident but by design, and therefore the preparations for Man's advent over the ages upon ages were signs which could be interpreted, if there was Mind to read them. One of the greatest of such signs was the movement of life out of the primeval waters onto the dry land.

Bible translators have not taken sufficient account of the root meaning of the Hebrew words when they rendered into English the commencement of the book of *Genesis*. It should read:

First of all God created heaven and earth.
But the earth was featureless and creatureless,
And a stillness lay upon the surface of the deep.
Only the Wind of God ruffled the surface of the waters.
Then God said, 'Let there be a stirring!'
And a stirring took place.
And God regarded the stirring and found it good.
So God distinguished stirring-time from still-time.
Stirring time He called Day, and still-time Night.
Thus passive and active was One Day.

As we have already noted, the ancient Jewish sages, commenting upon this, claimed that where it says "the Wind of God" that was the "Spirit of Messiah". The process which would culminate in the Messianic Age had already begun.

This optimistic attitude towards the creation argued that, while there might be many setbacks and long delays, in the end the Plan of God would be fulfilled, because who could defeat God's Will?

We are now at the beginning of an epoch of even greater significance than the movement of life on Earth out of water and onto dry land. We are at the beginning of the movement off the Earth out into space. This movement too, to reach its goal, may require a long period of time. Man will have to adapt to colonising the solar system, leaving the Earth as a holiday home to be visited for recreation.

Of old they looked for Signs of the Times, and so must we. Particularly we must observe how things are with the Jews. The revival of a State of Israel has been a remarkable sign, and no less the movement of Christianity towards seeking reconciliation with the Jews and a better understanding of Judaism. The participation of the Pope in a synagogue service has been a symbolic gesture in this respect, and quite noticeably Jewish scholars have been reclaiming Jesus for Israel.

There is still a long way to go. Christianity will have to abandon its paganism and return to its original Judaism. And Judaism must abandon its insularity, and return to its original Messianic universalism. Jesus must finally be understood and portrayed as a Jew, with recognisably semitic features. And this will be his real second advent. But we should not forget that in the Providence of God it was Romanism which was the instrument of preserving Christianity from extinction, and it was an isolationist Rabbinism which preserved Judaism from extinction. Both have served their purpose, and both have progressively to be abandoned. The God mankind must discover "has the whole world in His hand", and all religions of mankind must accommodate themselves ultimately to a new universalism, a partnership with God in His planetary programme.

A major move forward has even now to be made in the relationships between the former Communist Bloc and the Western Alliance. And it could be practicable if the hotheads and the obtuse were removed from the seats of power. At this stage ultimate reconciliation may yet be too much to hope for. They are likely in the foreseeable future to remain ideological rivals and industrial competitors. But it is a political fiction to say that nations have to be hell-bent on destroying each other. Consequently there is no requirement for them to protect themselves against each other with the most destructive lethal weapons ever invented, and which conceivably would spell ruination for all concerned, with a large part of the globe made uninhabitable for generations.

It is militarists who are the enemies of mankind in general, and it is they with their nuclear weapons who have to be ousted. These and other weapons are a drain on the economies of East and West, and thus an impediment to social progress.

Again there are indications that wiser counsels could prevail as an outcome of sensible discussions. If they should sufficiently succeed that too would be a sign of Messianic advance, a victory over the brutal and unfeeling. And it is in this connection that a People of God is sorely needed in a mediatorial and reconciling capacity.

Assuredly it lies within the capacity of man, once he is committed to the Divine Plan, to achieve his eventual apotheosis. The Messianic is an incentive mechanism, and the People of God has to be its central stimulus, the soul within the body.

# *Epilogue*

The aim of this book has been to link the prophetic to the historical, so that it can be seen that the story of Mankind, and indeed of our planet, is purposeful and objective. It is for us humans to discern why we are here, and progressively to identify ourselves with the Divine Plan, to put it into effect. We have to surrender "making it of no effect by our traditions".

This applies to Christians and Jews especially, as repositories of the Messianic; and it will be harder for Christians than for anyone else, since it means abandoning their most cherished and fundamental convictions. They are not used to seeing things in correct perspective, in historical perspective. They want everything in their Bible to be literally true, every recorded circumstance. They are still not prepared to see them in relation to the ideas and beliefs of a past age, in spite of the light thrown upon antique concepts through modern archaeological researches.

It has been my function to serve both the historical and the prophetic, and therefore to look at everything with a fresh insight. This book has been one outcome, and my sense of responsibility has been very great.

H. J. S.

# Index

141

Also published by OPEN GATE PRESS

HUGH J. SCHONFIELD

# Proclaiming the Messiah

THE LIFE AND LETTERS OF PAUL OF TARSUS,
ENVOY TO THE NATIONS

ISBN 1 871871 32 8    256pp    156 x 234 mm    p/b £9. 95
With 2 illustrations and 1 map

*Proclaiming the Messiah* shows conclusively that Paul was not, as Christians claim, the founder of a new religion, but a Jewish mystic who believed in the coming of the Messiah, whom he saw in Jesus. After many years of careful study Schonfield reached the conclusion that much of what is said about St Paul's writings stems from misunderstanding and partly deliberate misrepresentation. Schonfield's new translation, with notes and references, fully recognizes the Jewish religious ideas which lie behind the letters.

'... it is an unexpected delight to discover *Proclaiming the Messiah*,
a precious legacy of Hugh J. Schonfield. Schonfield's particular
array of convictions were, I say, unique in the ranks of New Testament
scholarship... distinctive views on Paul, his life and his doctrine...
fascinating notions. Schonfield's translation of the Pauline corpus makes
the familiar appear strange and new again... with its determined avoidance
of ecclesiastical jargon... word choices are often striking and refreshing...
documents stripped of their gilt edges and India paper, as if one were
getting a first glimpse of the Dead Sea Scrolls.'

Dr Robert M. Price, Editor, *Journal of Higher Criticism*